Praise for
RESURGENCE OF THE WAI

"This thoughtful book documents in valuable detail the myriad ways in which the tragedy of September 11 has been manipulated to justify militarism, wasteful government spending and a frightful increase in the power of the State. **Resurgence of the Warfare State** *is a serious book with a serious argument."*
> —**Alberto R. Coll**, Professor of Law, De Paul University and former Dean, U.S. Naval War College

"Robert Higgs's zesty, well-written book on the crisis after 9/11, **Resurgence of the Warfare State**, *righteously and rigorously flogs Bush and the feds time after time. His batterings of national security debacles remind readers of the folly of trusting Washington, now more than ever."*
> —**James Bovard**, author of *Lost Rights* and *Terrorism and Tyranny*

"Even those who do not share his views on government's proper role cannot fail to appreciate the many insightful elements of good sense in **Resurgence of the Warfare State**, *Robert Higgs's provocative and hard-hitting attack on the domestic implications of resurgent American interventionism."*
> —**Richard K. Betts**, Director, Institute of War and Peace Studies, Columbia University

"Robert Higgs is at his best in **Resurgence of the Warfare State**, *combining his broad knowledge of history and economics with a passion for liberty. Higgs provides a top-notch analysis of how the crusade for global democracy abroad and the related growth in the surveillance state at home threaten freedom and constitutional government. A highlight is how Higgs employs his mastery of history to hammer the point that freedoms 'temporarily' relinquished are rarely restored."*
> —**Ron Paul**, U.S. Congressman

"Robert Higgs challenges 'the warfare state' with analytical clarity and moral depth. His critique of American-style militarism is a solid rejection of the war-crazed obsessions that are propelling the vast majority of Washington's politicians and journalists. At its core, **Resurgence of the Warfare State** *is an intellectually cogent and ethically principled statement of opposition to the unhinged 'war on terrorism.'"*
> —**Norman Solomon**, author, *War Made Easy: How Presidents and Pundits Keep Spinning Us to Death*

"*Dr. Higgs has compiled an extraordinary, and extraordinarily timely, book for Americans and others who wish to understand post 9/11 America. Two hours spent in the pleasant company of this easy-to-read yet deeply concerned and insightful* **Resurgence of the Warfare State** *is a powerful education that will fortify patriots as it enrages statists. Required reading for all!*"

—**Lt. Col. Karen Kwiatkowski**, former Planning Staff Officer, Under Secretariat for Policy, U.S. Department of Defense

"*No one is as clear-headed and as wise on issues of war, peace, and government as Robert Higgs. I will give copies of his* **Resurgence of the Warfare State** *to all friends who are blinded by red, white, and blue hues.*"

—**Donald J. Boudreaux**, Professor of Economics, George Mason University

"**Resurgence of the Warfare State** *is a delight. Higgs is not only a distinguished economist and historian but a perceptive social critic. It is eerie to read Higgs's stunningly accurate predictions from 2002 and 2003 about the likely outcome of a war with Iraq and the 'war on terror.' You must read this incisive, biting, and quotable book.*"

—**David T. Beito**, Professor of History, University of Alabama

"*In* **Resurgence of the Warfare State**, *Higgs speaks truth to the power of the warfare state with the kind of spirited aggressiveness that is needed if truth is to prevail.*"

—**D. Gareth Porter**, author of *Perils of Dominance* and *The Road to War in Vietnam*

"*Robert Higgs is our foremost authority on the growth of government power through war and preparation for war. In his masterly analysis of the many dimensions of the currently metastasizing American warfare state, Higgs pulls no punches. His always spirited prose is a gust of fresh air to anyone exposed to the constant stream of clichés of the media. If you are able to read only one book on our deepening crisis,* **Resurgence of the Warfare State** *is the one you need.*"

—**Ralph Raico**, Professor of History, Buffalo State College

"*Robert Higgs's book on the events since 9/11,* **Resurgence of the Warfare State**, *demonstrates not just that war is the health of the state, but that it is also a disease to liberty. Those who believe that the wars on Iraq and 'terror' are compatible with a belief in limited government need to read this marvelous book.*"

—**Steven G. Horwitz**, Professor of Economics, St. Lawrence University

Resurgence of the Warfare State
The Crisis Since 9/11

Resurgence of the Warfare State

The Crisis Since 9/11

Robert Higgs

The INDEPENDENT INSTITUTE

Oakland, California

The Independent Institute
100 Swan Way, Oakland, CA 94621-1428
Telephone: 510-632-1366 • Fax: 510-568-6040
Email: info@independent.org
Website: www.independent.org

Library of Congress Cataloging-in-Publication Data

Higgs, Robert.
    Resurgence of the warfare state : the crisis since 9/11 / Robert Higgs.
        p. cm.

    ISBN-13: 978-0-945999-56-0 (pbk. : alk. paper)
    ISBN-10: 0-945999-56-9 (pbk. : alk. paper)

    1. United States–Politics and government–2001– 2. September 11 Terrorist Attacks, 2001–Influence. 3. War on Terrorism, 2001—Political aspects–United States. 4. Iraq War, 2003–Causes. 5. National security–United States. 6. Civil rights–United States. I. Independent Institute (Oakland, Calif.) II. Title.
    JK275.H54 2005
    320.973--dc22

                                                                        2005012003

    10 9 8 7 6 5 4 3 2 1   05 06 07 08 09

The INDEPENDENT INSTITUTE

THE INDEPENDENT INSTITUTE is a non-profit, non-partisan, scholarly research and educational organization that sponsors comprehensive studies of the political economy of critical social and economic issues.

The politicization of decision-making in society has too often confined public debate to the narrow reconsideration of existing policies. Given the prevailing influence of partisan interests, little social innovation has occurred. In order to understand both the nature of and possible solutions to major public issues, The Independent Institute's program adheres to the highest standards of independent inquiry and is pursued regardless of political or social biases and conventions. The resulting studies are widely distributed as books and other publications, and are publicly debated through numerous conference and media programs. Through this uncommon independence, depth, and clarity, The Independent Institute expands the frontiers of our knowledge, redefines the debate over public issues, and fosters new and effective directions for government reform.

Contents

Introduction   xi

PART I CRISIS AND LEVIATHAN, AGAIN   1

1 Glory Days for Government   3

2 Crisis Policymaking   9

3 Wake Up to the Law of the Ratchet   15

4 Every Step We Take   19

5 Crisis-Induced Losses of Liberties   21

6 Wartime Curbs on Liberty Are Costless?
   (It Just Ain't So!)   23

7 Benefits and Costs of the U.S. Government's
   War Making   27

PART II AIRPORT (IN)SECURITY   33

8 Federal Oversight Won't Improve Airport Security   35

9 The Pretense of Airport Security   37

PART III THE DRAFT   41

10 Will the Draft Rise from the Dead?   43

11 Censored Mail   45

PART IV THE POLITICAL ECONOMY OF THE MILITARY-INDUSTRIAL-CONGRESSIONAL COMPLEX 47

12 The Cold War 49

13 U.S. National Security 55

14 The Government Needs to Get Its Own Accounting House in Order 59

15 Nation Trembles as Congress Reassembles 63

16 If We're Really in Danger, Why Doesn't the Government Act as if We're in Danger? 67

17 Free Enterprise and War, a Dangerous Liaison 73

18 War Prosperity 79

19 Suppose You Wanted to Have a Permanent War 81

20 How Does the War Party Get Away with It? 87

21 The Defense Budget Is Bigger Than You Think 93

PART V BUSH AND THE BUSHIES 97

22 The President Is Reading a Book, I'm Afraid 99

23 George Bush's Faith-Based Foreign Policy 103

24 On Crackpot Realism 107

25 Camelot and the Bushies 111

26 Is Bush Unhinged? 117

PART VI THE ROAD TO WAR 123

27 Iraq and the United States 125

28 Helplessly, We Await the Catastrophe Our Rulers Are Creating 129

29 To Make War, Presidents Lie 133

30 Saddam Hussein Can't Blackmail Us with a
Fissionable Softball 137

31 Why the Rush to War? 141

32 Paul Craig Roberts Interviews
Robert Higgs on War and Liberty 145

33 Nuke France 149

PART VII SLAUGHTERING THE INNOCENT 153

34 Collateral Damage 155

35 Military Precision versus Moral Precision 159

36 Some Are Weeping, Some Are Not 163

37 Are Pro-war Libertarians Right? 167

38 Not Exactly an Eye for an Eye 171

39 Defense of Your Home Is Not Terrorism,
Not Even in Iraq 175

40 What's So Special About Those Killed by
Hijackers on September 11, 2001? 179

41 The Crimes at Abu Ghraib Are Not the Worst 183

42 Has the U.S. Government Committed
War Crimes in Afghanistan and Iraq? 191

PART VIII CAKE WALK 197

43 WMD Blues 199

44 Taking Stock One Year after the
U.S. Invasion of Iraq 203

45 Can Bullets and Bombs Establish Justice in Iraq? 211

46 Bush's Iraq War   217

47 The Iraq War—A Catastrophic Success   223

    Acknowledgments   229

    Further Reading   237

    Index   239

    About the Author   251

Introduction

Only a few days after the infamous events of September 11, 2001, journalists and public-policy organizations began to contact me seeking my views with regard to the likely consequences. They sought my opinion because they knew about my book *Crisis and Leviathan: Critical Episodes in the Growth of American Government* (Oxford University Press, 1987) and about other published studies I had carried out and lectures I had given on related subjects over the previous twenty years. Believing that knowledge of historical patterns might indeed help us to understand better the government's response to the attacks, I agreed to answer questions and to write brief commentaries for several think tanks. My early statements appeared in *Reason* magazine, *Reason Online*, the *National Post* (Canada), the *Financial Times* (London), the *Wall Street Journal*, and the Foundation for Economic Education's monthly *Ideas on Liberty*, as well as in a brief analysis for the National Center for Policy Analysis. I also spoke with reporters for the *New York Times* and the Voice of America, appeared on several talk-radio shows, and taped interviews for PBS Television broadcasts of *The McCuistion Program* and *Uncommon Knowledge*. Little did I realize, however, that these contributions would be only the opening chapter of a continuing engagement that has now stretched more than three and a half years—and seems likely to go on indefinitely.

As time passed, I had occasion to write and to speak about a wide range of events, institutions, and persons somehow related to the U.S. responses to the 9/11 attacks, both at home and abroad. I commented on airport-security measures; proposals to reinstate the military draft; the doings of the leading actors in the military-industrial-congressional complex as well as the operation of the larger political economy in which it is embedded; George W. Bush and his administration; the U.S. government's actions and statements during the run-up to the March 2003 invasion and subsequent occupation of Iraq; the extensive "collateral damage" wreaked on noncombatants in Afghanistan and Iraq; the catastrophic outcome of the war for many people caught up in it and its lawless, violent aftermath; and the great political and material success enjoyed by the principal U.S. architects of the war and by their chief supporters and cronies. In various magazines and leading newspapers, especially the *San Francisco Chronicle,* and at various Web sites, especially LewRockwell.com and independent.org, I produced a running stream of analysis and evaluation.

I eventually produced dozens of statements, commentaries, and other forms of expression, including some poems and satires, on these topics. Many were reproduced or hyperlinked at various Web sites, where they evoked considerable comment and discussion, and were reprinted in hard-copy publications not only in this country but in Europe, Australia, New Zealand, Latin America, and Asia, sometimes in translation to the local language. This reception suggested that an even wider audience might exist for these materials and that if brought together, they might be seen to compose something greater than the sum of their parts. Hence, the collection in this volume.

It seemed at first that the best presentation scheme would be a strictly chronological ordering of the various pieces. Placed in the order of their appearance, they would constitute a series of now-and-again entries similar to those in an irregularly kept diary. Although this plan continued to appeal to me, publisher David Theroux persuaded me that a better plan would be to group the pieces into a few general subject categories. Therefore, such a grouping has been made here, but within each category, the pieces appear in the order of their dates of publication or other issuance. This arrangement should help the reader to place each piece in the appropriate context of what had happened already, what was happening concurrently, and what was being affirmed or denied at the time by various parties. In keeping with the spirit of the presentation scheme, the pieces appear here exactly as they appeared originally, except for the correction of a few minor mistakes, the clarification of a few ambiguities, and the standardization of the spelling and usage of certain words (such as *al Qaeda* and *USA PATRIOT Act*).

I took no pleasure in following these events or in writing and speaking about them, nor did I profit financially. Apart from a small honorarium that I received from the National Center for Policy Analysis for an article that the center invited me to write, I received no payment for the articles, interviews, and other materials included here. I acted solely as a human being who has an interest in whether other human beings suffer injustice: when I hear the bell tolling, I know that it tolls for me. I harbored no illusions, however, that by speaking out I might somehow alter the course of events. If I had any comprehensible motive other than to express my disgust with the U.S. government's actions, it was simply, as the Christians say, to bear witness: to leave some scraps of evidence that while these great crimes were being committed, I did not remain silent.

Although I have engaged in scholarly study of many of the subjects discussed here and therefore everything I now say about them reflects what I have learned from a lifetime of study, this book is not a work of scholarship. It contains commentaries and statements intended for a lay audience: no footnotes and no extensive bibliography, only a brief list of recommended readings at the end. Because I presumed that my readers or listeners had no special knowledge or expertise in these areas, I sometimes put on my old professorial hat and engaged in a bit of remedial instruction. I make no apology for having done so; in large part, the present political situation in the United States has come about because the public is ignorant of many important facts and relationships and therefore is easily misled by interested parties, especially by the president of the United States and those under his command, most of all in relation to questions of war and peace.

The ideal of scholarship is dispassionate, "value-free" analysis. The reader will not find that kind of writing here. Although, as just mentioned, my scholarship has informed my understanding in countless ways, I have made no attempt here to suppress or to conceal my own values. Indeed, perhaps my greatest grievance during the past four years has been that the values I hold dearest—justice, peace, humanity, honesty, and basic decency—have been savaged most fiercely.

At every step, of course, the perpetrators have boldly proclaimed that black is white; that the road to peace must be paved with gravestones; that the "reconstruction" of a city or even an entire country begins by obliterating it with bombs, rockets, shells, and bullets; that "liberation" takes the form of heavily armed soldiers bursting into homes and mosques and dragging people off to torture them in hideous prisons, then blaming everything on "terrorists" who include, it turns out, little children now with their eyes blinded, their skin burned, or their limbs blown off by U.S. bombs and bullets. If George Orwell were alive today, he would not be surprised, but he would surely have plenty of fresh raw material for his continuing analysis of Newspeak. To listen to political leaders' pronouncements at any time requires a strong stomach, but during the past four years the challenge has often been greater than I could bear. How anyone can actually admire these people surpasses my powers of comprehension.

Here, then, is one man's responses to a series of events and to the decisions made by those who purport to be his rulers. To say that I have looked upon the emperor in his allegedly resplendent attire and found him to be naked does not even begin to capture my verdict. Of course, I do not represent my statements to be the last word on anything. Much of the commentary here represents my reaction to events as they unfolded, when the fog of war and propaganda still lay heavily over the terrain. Naturally, I may have misapprehended things here and there. Unlike the emperor, I am not infallible; I do not receive messages directly from God; and I do not possess the advantages of a $40-billion-a-year intelligence apparatus to help me get at the truth. What excuse, I wonder, does the emperor have?

Robert Higgs
Covington, Louisiana
April 2, 2005

PART I

Crisis and Leviathan, Again

1 | Glory Days for Government

An Economic Historian Talks about National-Security Crises and the Growth of Government

Michael Lynch of Reason *interviews Robert Higgs shortly after 9/11.*

As Operation Infinite Justice gets under way, the war drums are beating across the land, and a battle will surely come, although we know neither when nor what particular form it will take. Only this much is certain: though our government didn't bring on last week's terrorist attacks and everyone in Washington would certainly give plenty for them not to have occurred, war is a great friend of the state. In such troubled times, people look to the federal government for action and assurance. To get predictions about what we might expect to happen this time around, I checked in with economic historian Robert Higgs, whose book *Crisis And Leviathan* (Oxford University Press, 1987) insightfully chronicled how national crises in the twentieth century consistently helped grow the size and scope of our federal government. Higgs is a senior fellow in political economy at the Independent Institute and editor of the institute's quarterly journal *The Independent Review.*

REASON: What's the thesis of your book?

ROBERT HIGGS: In a nutshell, it's that when a crisis of major significance occurs—something as large-scale and pervasive as the Great Depression or the world wars—there's an overwhelming public demand for government to act. In the twentieth century, every national emergency has seen federal government take unprecedented action to somehow allay the perceived threat to our security. These actions have taken a great many forms, but the common denominator is that they all entail the increased exercise of power by government over society and the economy. When the crisis ends, many of the emergency actions cease. But not all of them. Each emergency ratchets up the size and scope of the federal government. In some cases, agencies that had a very strict relation to the emergency transform to take on new missions.

REASON: What's an example of an agency that transformed itself?

HIGGS: The War Finance Corporation in World War I was created to provide funds for various munitions enterprises. When the war ended, the War Finance Corporation turned to financing agricultural cooperatives and the export of agricultural products to Europe. It lived on until 1925. In 1932, it was revived to bail out railroads and other big companies that were going bankrupt during the Great Depression. During World War II, it was used for a multitude of new missions, including building new defense plants and stockpiling defense materials. When it was finally abolished in the 1950s because of scandals, it was immediately re-created in part as the Small Business Administration, which itself has taken on a variety of tasks over time.

REASON: Are the attacks on the World Trade Center and the Pentagon a large enough crisis to feed Leviathan?

HIGGS: It's a big enough perceived emergency to cause the government to extend into areas it may not have moved into so quickly, particularly surveillance of ordinary citizens and ordinary locations where people might congregate for business or recreational purposes.

REASON: Is it appropriate for individuals to worry about government expanding at this time?

HIGGS: It's extremely appropriate, because historically a large proportion of all government expansion has taken place as an emergency or crisis action. It's precisely under conditions such as those that exist at present that we ought to worry the most about the expansion of government.

REASON: What ought we to look for this time?

HIGGS: We can expect thousands of reservists to be called to active duty and taken away from their ordinary jobs. We can expect the assignment of military forces to some unprecedented duties. It appears that some military units are going to be used for domestic police activities. It is clearly going to be the case that the FBI will become far more active in surveillance activities. The government will mount a variety of overseas actions requiring the armed forces, and perhaps a number of civilian employees, to attempt to kill, to disable, or to damage what are taken to be terrorist cadres, camps, or facilities. It is also fairly clear that the government is going to have to bail out the airline industry and maybe the insurance industry. When the government takes large-scale, unprecedented actions of this sort, unanticipated consequences always occur. Then the government has to expand even further to deal with those consequences.

REASON: Civil liberties always take a beating in war. Do the restrictions recede after wars are over?

HIGGS: The civil liberties violations during the world wars were, for the most part, abandoned after the wars, but not entirely. But they left institutional residues and changes in public attitudes and outlooks that could be exploited afterward. For example, it's pretty clear that World War I hysteria directed at the Germans was later directed at individuals caught up in the so-called Red Scare. People were already in a high state of excitement about "un-Americanism." That was instrumental in the ability of the government to persecute, deport, and otherwise harm a number of foreigners who were in the country at that time. The FBI expanded during World War II. After the war, FBI activities were often directed at dissident political factions, especially in the 1960s. Wars have increased state power both directly and indirectly. I've been talking about fairly direct ways in which the government changed opinions and institutions to enable it to do new things after a crisis ended. But a very important way in which both world wars enlarged the power of government was through the effect on government budgets. We can see that same effect operating now. Governments at war spend much more money than they otherwise would. In doing so, normal constraints on government spending are broken—particularly people's attitudes about the importance of balancing the budget or belief that no more than x dollars ought to be spent for a certain purpose. Both world wars caused the size of government relative to gross domestic product to take a jump up, and there was never retrenchment to the relative levels before the wars. We see something similar in the current episode. Until recently there was a great deal of political struggle over not spending the supposed Social Security surplus. As soon as the crisis burst forth, that concern evaporated. Congress gave the president twice as much money as he asked for when he went in for an emergency appropriation. That is pretty much in character with past crises. Fiscal constraints break down very quickly in the face of perceived emergency conditions.

REASON: What's the nature of the coming crisis?

HIGGS: The whole concept of wiping out terrorism is completely misguided. It simply can't be done. Terrorism is a simple act for any determined adult to perpetrate no matter what kind of security measures are taken. I suspect that after the government finishes making its show [of force] in the next few weeks, it will only inspire new acts of terrorism—if not immediately, then eventually. If the government were really serious about diminishing the amount of effective terrorist acts, it would set about creating a global corps of truly unsavory informants on the ground. But it's never shown in the past that it's had the wit to do that. I don't expect it to have the wit to do it this time. I expect to see a lot of huffing and puffing, calling up troops, dropping bombs and missiles, and maybe this time even sending in special forces for attacks on one group or another. But this is all politics. It's not going to make a dent in the genuine threat of terrorism.

REASON: What do you expect in terms of Leviathan at the end of the day?

HIGGS: The ultimate result will be an enlargement of the Big Brother State. We were moving that way already. This will accelerate it.

Michael W. Lynch is Reason's *national correspondent.*

2

Crisis Policymaking
Immediate Action, Prolonged Regret

In a national emergency, perhaps the strongest urge of democratically elected officials is to "do something" immediately. Politicians believe that inaction sends citizens the message that their leaders are indecisive and perhaps incompetent to deal with the crisis. In the wake of the September 11 terrorist attacks, Congress and the president are proposing a host of new security measures and other laws and regulations. Federal spending—which, as figure 1 shows, spiked for both World Wars—is about to spike again with higher spending for the military, domestic security, stricken industries, and perhaps other items.

FIGURE 1 Total Government Current Expenditures as a Percentage of Gross Domestic Product 1900–1999. Source: Historical Statistics 1999.

In America's past, however, in virtually every case, policies adopted in the heat of the moment have proven, in cool retrospect, to have been overreactions that sapped the long-term vitality of civil society and the free-market economy.

WORLD WAR I

With U.S. entry into World War I, the federal government expanded enormously in size, scope, and power. It virtually nationalized the ocean shipping industry. It did nationalize the railroad, telephone, domestic telegraph, and international telegraphic cable industries. It became deeply engaged in manipulating labor-management relations, securities sales, agricultural production and marketing, the distribution of coal and oil, international commerce, and markets for raw materials and manufactured products. Its Liberty Bond drives dominated the financial capital markets. It turned the newly created Federal Reserve System into a powerful engine of monetary inflation to help satisfy the government's voracious appetite for money and credit. In view of the more than five thousand mobilization agencies of various sorts—boards, committees, corporations, and administrations—contemporaries who described the 1918 government as "war socialism" were well justified.

To ensure that the conscription-based mobilization of an army could proceed without obstruction, the government had to silence its critics. The Espionage Act of June 15, 1917, penalized those convicted of willfully obstructing the enlistment services with fines of up to $10,000 and imprisonment of as long as twenty years. An amendment, the Sedition Act of May 16, 1918, went much further, imposing the same severe criminal penalties on all forms of expression in any way critical of the government, its symbols, or its mobilization of resources for the war. Those suppressions of free speech, subsequently upheld by the Supreme Court, established dangerous precedents that derogated from the rights previously enjoyed by citizens under the First Amendment.

The government further subverted the Bill of Rights by censoring all printed materials, peremptorily deporting hundreds of aliens without due process of law and conducting—and encouraging state and local governments and vigilante groups to conduct—warrantless searches and seizures, blanket arrests of suspected draft evaders, and other outrages too numerous to catalog here. In California, the police arrested Upton Sinclair for reading the Bill of Rights at a rally. In New Jersey, the police arrested Roger Baldwin for publicly reading the Constitution.

When the war ended, the government abandoned most, but not all, of its wartime control measures. By the end of 1920, the bulk of the economic regulatory apparatus had been scrapped, including the Food Administration, the Fuel Administration, the Railroad Administration, the War Industries Board, and the War Labor Board. Some emergency powers migrated into regular government departments such as State, Labor, and Treasury and continued in force. The Espionage Act and the Trading with the Enemy Act remained on the statute books. Congressional enactments in 1920 preserved much of the federal government's wartime involvement in the railroad and ocean shipping industries. The War Finance Corporation shifted missions, subsidizing exporters and farmers until the mid-1920s. Wartime prohibition of alcoholic beverages, a purported conservation measure, transmogrified into the ill-fated Eighteenth Amendment.

WORLD WAR II

During World War II, federal authorities resorted to a vast system of controls and market interventions to get resources without having to bid them away from competing buyers in free markets. By fixing prices, directly allocating physical and human resources, establishing official priorities, prohibitions, and set-asides, then rationing the civilian consumer goods in short supply, the war planners steered raw materials, intermediate goods, and finished products into the uses they valued most. Markets no longer functioned freely; in many areas they did not function at all.

World War II witnessed massive violations of human rights in the United States. Most egregiously, some 112,000 blameless persons of Japanese ancestry, most of them U.S. citizens, were uprooted from their homes and confined in concentration camps without due process of law. Those subsequently released as civilians during the war remained under parolelike surveillance. The government also imprisoned nearly 6,000 conscientious objectors—three-fourths of them Jehovah's Witnesses—who would not comply with the military draft laws. Signaling the enlarged federal capacity for repression, the number of FBI special agents increased from 785 in 1939 to 4,370 in 1945.

Scores of newspapers were denied the privilege of the mails under the authority of the 1917 Espionage Act, which remained in effect. Some newspapers were banned altogether. The Office of Censorship restricted the content of press reports and radio broadcasts and censored personal mail entering or leaving the country.

The government seized more than sixty industrial facilities—sometimes entire industries (e.g., railroads, bituminous coal mines, meatpacking firms)—most of them in order to impose employment conditions favorable to labor unions engaged in disputes with the management.

At the end of the war, most of the economic control agencies shut down. Some powers persisted, however, either lodged at the local level, like New York City's rent controls, or shifted from emergency agencies to regular departments. For example, certain international-trade controls were moved from the wartime Foreign Economic Administration to the State Department.

Federal tax revenues remained very high by prewar standards. In the late 1940s, the Internal Revenue Service's annual take averaged four times greater in constant dollars than in the late 1930s. In 1949, federal outlays amounted to 15 percent of gross national product, up from 10 percent in 1939. The national debt stood at what would have been an unthinkable figure before the war, $214 billion—in constant dollars, roughly one hundred times the national debt in 1916.

THE COLD WAR

During the Cold War, the government's operatives committed crimes against the American people too numerous to catalog here. The government's reprehensible actions, which many citizens viewed as only abuses, we can apprehend more plausibly as intrinsic to its constant preparation for and episodic engagement in warfare.

CONCLUSION

President Bush and his subordinates proclaim that the United States has entered into "a new kind of war." Unfortunately, this undertaking has the potential for the same kind of domestic abuses and excesses associated with previous U.S. wars. Already some officials have proposed such steps as requiring everyone to carry a national identification card, allowing the indefinite detention of legal immigrants without charges or hearings, and vastly increasing government surveillance powers. Because policies once established are so difficult to reform or abolish, it behooves everyone to act with deliberation during the present crisis. To act rashly, as if our present reactions to the attacks of September 11 posed no long-term dangers to the very liberties we seek to protect, would be to repeat history in the worst way.

3 | Wake Up to the Law of the Ratchet

National Emergencies Attract Opportunists Who Seek to Profit from the Growth of Government, Say Steve Hanke and Robert Higgs

As the United States confronts a new crisis, the opportunists are once again playing the system and exploiting it for their own ends.

Much of the growth of government in the United States and elsewhere occurs as a direct or indirect result of national emergencies such as wars and economic depressions.

Laws are enacted, bureaus are created, and budgets are enlarged. In many cases, these changes turn out to be permanent. The result is that crises act as a ratchet, shifting the trend line of government's size and scope up to a higher level.

It comes as no surprise that governments spend more money and regulate more actively during crises—wars and economic bailouts are expensive and complicated. But a more active government also attracts opportunists who perceive that a national emergency can serve as a useful pretext for achieving their own objectives.

The United States and other countries seem no more aware of this today than they were in the past. And yet history has provided many examples to illustrate how damaging it is.

Take the Great Depression. At that time, the organized farm lobbies, having sought subsidies for decades, took advantage of the crisis to pass a sweeping rescue package, the Agricultural Adjustment Act, whose title declared it to be "an act to relieve the existing national economic emergency."

Almost seventy years later, the farmers are still sucking money from the rest of society, and agricultural policy has been enlarged to satisfy a variety of other interest groups, including conservationists, nutritionists, and friends of the Third World.

Originally appeared November 26, 2001

Then, during the Second World War, when government accounted for nearly half the U.S. gross domestic product, virtually every interest group tried to tap into the vastly enlarged government budget. Even bureaus seemingly remote from the war effort, such as the Department of the Interior, claimed to be performing "essential war work" and to be entitled to bigger budgets and more personnel.

Smaller crises have sent the opportunists into feeding frenzies, too. The ever-opportunistic International Monetary Fund (IMF) is a classic case. Established as part of the 1944 Bretton Woods agreement, the IMF was responsible primarily for extending short-term, subsidized credits to countries experiencing balance-of-payments problems under the postwar pegged-exchange-rate system. In 1971, however, Richard Nixon, then U.S. president, closed the gold window, signaling the collapse of the Bretton Woods agreement and, presumably, the demise of the IMF's original purpose. But since then the IMF has used every so-called crisis to expand its scope and scale.

The oil crises of the 1970s allowed the institution to reinvent itself. Those shocks required more IMF lending to facilitate, yes, balance-of-payments adjustments. And more lending there was: from 1970 to 1975, IMF lending more than doubled in real terms; from 1975 to 1982, it increased by 58 percent in real terms.

With the election of Ronald Reagan as U.S. president in 1980, it seemed the IMF's crisis-driven opportunism might be reined in. Yet with the onset of the Mexican debt crisis, more IMF lending was "required" to prevent debt crises and bank failures. That rationale was used by none other than President Ronald Reagan, who personally lobbied 400 out of 435 congressmen to obtain approval for a U.S. quota increase for the IMF. IMF lending ratcheted up again, increasing 27 percent in real terms during Mr. Reagan's first term in office.

Not surprisingly, the events of September 11 did not catch the IMF flat-footed. On September 18, Paul O'Neill, the U.S. Treasury secretary, had breakfast with Horst Kohler, the IMF's managing director, to discuss the financial needs of coalition partners. Also on their agenda was the IMF's denial of funds to countries that failed to toe Washington's line.

Within the U.S. government, the latest emergency has given cover to a multitude of parochial opportunists whose proposals range from bailing out the airlines to nationalizing vaccine production. The resulting "stimulus package" amounts to about Dollars 100bn (Pounds 70bn).

The ratchet continues to operate on ideology, too. A recent poll conducted by the *Washington Post* indicates that 53 percent of Americans think the government "is run for the benefit of all the people," up from 35 percent last year. Only 37 percent agreed that "the government is pretty much run by a few big interests looking out for themselves," the lowest percentage since 1966, when 33 percent embraced that view.

It may be too much to expect a speedy end to the law of the ratchet, but it is time to acknowledge what is going on. That, at least, may make it easier to reverse the trend during times of stability.

Coauthored with Steve Hanke, who is a professor of applied economics at the Johns Hopkins University, research fellow at the Independent Institute, and chairman of the Friedberg Mercantile Group in New York.

4

Every Step We Take

The American people may well be witnessing the death of their right to privacy, not with their usual whimper but with their ill-considered, too-hasty approval after the New York and Pentagon bangs.

The government has declared war on "terrorism," but because terrorists assume many guises and operate in many places, the only way to ensure that no terrorist escapes notice is to watch everyone, everywhere. Lacking the patience and the wit to focus its surveillance on only the most likely suspects, the government will regard all of us as potential terrorists or as their potential providers, unwitting perhaps, of aid and comfort. Our communications by ordinary mail, telephone, fax, and e-mail will be scrutinized or at constant risk of scrutiny; our homes and places of business will be searched or at constant risk of search; our personal contacts, financial affairs, and travel by airliner, train, and ship will be closely monitored and restricted. To borrow the lyrics of a once-popular song: "Every step we take / every move we make / they'll be watching us."

Of course, once people have been subjected to such thoroughgoing government surveillance, all relations between the government and the public are transformed. Whether the rulers be revolutionary despots or democratically elected officials, every citizen knows that "they" know all about him and his affairs, and hence no one dares to step out of line. In such a situation, the sociopolitical system will gravitate ineluctably toward totalitarianism.

Originally appeared December 2001

5

Crisis-Induced Losses of Liberties

To the Editor, the *Wall Street Journal*:

Michael Barone thinks that, this time, war will not give rise to significant increases in the size and scope of government ("Not a Victory for Big Government," editorial page, January 15), because the war on terrorism does not require the massive spending and comprehensive economic controls of World War II, and because the voters continue, at least in certain polls, to favor smaller government in the abstract.

Having studied this topic for a long time and written a book on it (*Crisis and Leviathan,* Oxford University Press, 1987), I am not convinced that the present crisis will differ from the previous ones, all of which, from World War I through the civil rights/Vietnam War episode, did cause a permanent upsurge of government.

Because the war on terrorism has just begun, it is too soon to conclude that the pattern that held throughout the twentieth century has been broken. If the government decides to wage a full-scale war against Iraq, as a number of high-level officials and advisers are urging, or if it sends forces to fight on a front stretching from Africa to Indonesia to the Philippines, then the size and scope of government will certainly grow.

Already, however, the government has grown in significant ways. Especially important are the greatly enhanced powers the government has assumed to spy on and seize the property of all Americans. Several parts of the USA PATRIOT Act bulk up the Big Brother State, from sneak-and-peak provisions to asset-confiscation measures ostensibly aimed at abating money laundering—the latter premised on evidence inadmissible in U.S. courts.

Attorney General John Ashcroft has reactivated the FBI's notorious COINTELPRO operation used from 1957 to 1971 to spy on domestic political and religious organizations. A number of states are considering the enactment of emergency laws that would give their governors draconian powers over persons, property, and personal information.

As such measures continue to augment the government's powers at all levels, the population remains in large part insensitive to the threats those measures pose to liberty, not just now but in all likelihood for many years to come. Pollster John Zogby declared recently that "the willingness to give up personal liberties is stunning, because the level of fear is so high." We can only hope that people regain their composure and their sense of proportion before the ratchet turns once again and our liberties sustain another irreversible crisis-induced loss.

6

Wartime Curbs on Liberty Are Costless? (It Just Ain't So!)

In one of the most provocative opinion articles of recent times, "Security Comes before Liberty" (*Wall Street Journal,* October 23, 2001), Jay Winik argued (1) that in previous national emergencies, U.S. presidents took strong repressive measures against citizens and other residents of the country, (2) that the repressive measures implemented so far by the Bush administration are comparatively mild, and (3) that notwithstanding the more draconian measures taken during previous crises, "normalcy returned, and so too did civil liberties, invariably stronger than before." Hence, Winik concluded, even if the Bush administration "deems it necessary to enact more restrictive steps, we need not fear."

Several commentators quickly took issue with Winik's argument. Most important, the critics challenged the claim that "despite these previous and numerous extreme measures, there was little long-term or corrosive effect on society after the security threat had subsided." In fact, each episode of national emergency left the liberties of Americans not "stronger than before," but severely maimed and weakened.

During World War I, the Wilson administration took sweeping actions to suppress not only individuals' freedom of action, but even their freedom of expression. The 1918 Sedition Act must be read to be believed. Under it, one might be, as some two thousand persons were, prosecuted for daring to "utter, print, write, or publish any disloyal, profane, scurrilous, or abusive language about the form of government of the United States, or the Constitution of the United States, or the military or naval forces of the United States, or the flag of the United States, or the uniform of the Army or Navy of the United States, or any language intended to bring the form of government of the United States, or the Constitution of the United States, or the military or naval forces of the United States, or the flag of the United States, or the uniform of the Army or Navy of the United Sates into contempt, scorn, contumely, or disrepute." Nor was this all the statute forbade!

When convictions under the Sedition Act were challenged in the courts, the U.S. Supreme Court upheld the statute. To his eternal shame, Justice Oliver Wendell Holmes Jr. wrote: "When a nation is at war, many things that might be said in time of peace are such a hindrance to its effort that their utterance will not be endured so long as men fight and no Court could regard them as protected by any constitutional right." This decision and others upholding unconstitutional measures undertaken by the Wilson administration might strike the proverbial Man from Mars as odd because the Constitution itself makes no provision for its own evisceration during wartime or other crisis, yet time and again during national emergencies the justices have allowed the legislative branch and especially the executive branch of government to transcend their constitutionally enumerated powers and to nullify individual rights proclaimed in the Constitution.

The Wilson administration conscripted some 2.8 million men—70 percent of those who served in the army. The Supreme Court could find no constitutional infirmity in that involuntary servitude, and its ruling has been a decisive precedent for judges ever since. The government also intervened massively in economic affairs, setting prices, allocating raw materials, and even going so far as to nationalize the interstate railroad, ocean shipping, and telecommunications industries. Those measures established precedents that would return to haunt subsequent generations and undercut their liberties in later crises—economic depressions as well as wars—each time entering more deeply into the fiber of American life, with malign effects on the traditional American devotion to liberty.

World War II became the occasion for unprecedented repressive actions by the U.S. government. More than 10 million young men—about 63 percent of all those who served in the armed forces during the war—were drafted to fight, and hundreds of thousands of them died or suffered serious wounds. The government imprisoned nearly 6,000 conscientious objectors, most of them Jehovah's Witnesses, who refused to obey the conscription laws. Totally without due process of law, the government confined some 112,000 innocent persons of Japanese ancestry, most of them U.S. citizens, in concentration camps in desolate areas of the west. Perceived enemies of FDR's administration came under surveillance by the FBI, whose special-agent ranks mushroomed from 785 to 4,370 during the war.

The government built a massive apparatus of economic controls between 1941 and 1945 and displaced free markets for the duration. No one should pooh-pooh the wartime economic controls because they entailed a sacrifice of "mere" economic liberties as opposed to "precious" civil liberties. Men were sent to prison for violating price controls, and people were displaced from their homes to make way for military construction projects. Wartime taxation itself was no trivial assault.

To pay for the gargantuan munitions production, the government imposed new taxes and raised the rates of existing taxes to unprecedented heights. Payroll withholding of income taxes was instituted, as portentous an action as any, because it created a virtually automatic means of snatching people's earnings and thereby greatly facilitated the government's subsequent financing of its ever-growing expenditures. Despite the vastly increased taxation, the government had to borrow most of its wartime revenue, and the national debt swelled by $200 billion (equivalent to roughly ten times that amount in today's dollars), or about fivefold, creating liabilities that would hover over taxpayers ever afterward.

CAN-DO GOVERNMENT

World War II gave a tremendous fillip to the federal government's reputation as a "can-do" organization, which helped to sustain various wartime economic controls, most notoriously New York City's never-abandoned rent controls. Moreover, as economist Calvin Hoover observed, the war "conditioned [American businessmen] to accept a degree of governmental intervention and control after the war which they had deeply resented prior to it."

During the prolonged Cold War emergency, an apprehensive nation grew accustomed to extensive domestic surveillance, government infiltration of dissident political groups, and even the murder of persons perceived by the government as threats to "national security." In the light of these and countless other facts, one wonders how Winik managed to conclude that "our democracy can, and has, outlived temporary restrictions and continued to thrive"?

Winik would have us believe that even if the government should adopt much more repressive measures to fight its declared "war on terrorism"—and indeed it has done so since his article appeared—we shall ultimately get past them, back to our glorious democracy, with the dangers surmounted and our freedoms undiminished. Vice President Dick Cheney, however, sees the matter in a different light. The present war "may never end," Cheney said on October 19. "It's a new normalcy."

In the weeks that have passed since the vice president uttered those ominous words, the government has continued to act in ways that confirm the worst fears of those who cherish a free society. Many of the measures being taken will have little effect on terrorism, but much effect on ordinary Americans, and many of those measures will surely persist even when the present crisis has passed.

7

Benefits and Costs of the U.S. Government's War Making

In 1795, James Madison observed that "of all the enemies to public liberty, war is, perhaps, the most to be dreaded, because it comprises and develops the germ of every other. . . . No nation could preserve its freedom in the midst of continual warfare." All experience during the past two centuries has confirmed the continuing validity of Madison's observation. Apart from all the sacrifices of life, liberty, and treasure that wars have entailed directly, they have also served as the prime occasions for the growth of the central state, and hence in the United States they have fostered the long-term diminution of civil and economic liberties and the ongoing subversion of civil society.

Every government recognizes that force alone is an inefficient means of propping up its position. At the margin, bamboozlement can be effectively substituted for the use of force, especially in so-called democratic systems, where many ordinary people have embraced the fable that they themselves "are" the government because they cast a ballot every few years. Hence, every government seeks to ease its retention of power by persuading people that it acts only in their interest. A government that goes to war promises its subjects that it is doing so only in defense of those persons' security and freedom. "Yet," as Bruce D. Porter has noted, "having borne the burden of the state for five hundred years, we find that it has rarely fulfilled its twin promises of security and freedom."

Indeed, the government's alluring claim is almost always false. In matters of war making, as elsewhere in their wielding of power, governments act in the interest of their own leaders, with as many concessions as necessary to retain the support of the coalition of special-interest groups that keeps them in power. Libertarians, of all people, understand that, in Randolph Bourne's now-hackneyed phrase, "war is the health of the state." This claim is not some wild-eyed ideological pronouncement; it is as well established as any historical regularity can be. Entire books, such as Porter's *War and the Rise of the State* (1994) and my own *Crisis and Leviathan* (1987) and *Against Leviathan* (2004), have documented it in excruciating detail.

Aware of this reality, libertarians instinctively resist any claim that war will promote either liberty or security; they do not expect that notwithstanding what has almost always happened before, nature will change its course on this particular occasion. Whereas many other people can be persuaded that the risks war poses to their own life, liberty, and property rights are justified—necessary and only temporary sacrifices in the service of their own long-term security and liberty—libertarians understand that those who embrace this logic are taking a gamble against very long odds.

In the United States, the government has been at war, more or less, since 1940, which is to say, in Madison's phrase, engaged in "continual warfare" or in massive preparation for warfare. Can anyone seriously maintain that we are now freer or more secure than we were *before* the sainted Franklin D. Roosevelt and his spiritual descendants took command of the ship of state and steered it into the storm of perpetual war? The U.S. government, which once confined its foreign adventures to ad hoc interventions, most of them in small Caribbean and Central American countries, has acted ever since World War II as a globe-girdling empire, projecting U.S. military and political power here, there, and everywhere with reckless unconcern for a reasonable connection between overall cost and benefit. (Why *should* the rulers care, you may ask, when they themselves—and, as usual, their supporting cronies—reap whatever benefit is produced, whereas the costs of the interventions take the form of other people's sacrifices of life, liberty, and property rights?)

Not least among these sacrifices has been that of the old constitutional structure—the government of checks and balances that once helped to restrain the rulers from launching foreign engage-ments and suppressing domestic liberties willy-nilly. Owing to the series of hot and cold military emergencies since 1940, the president has become, for all practical purposes, a Caesar. He now goes to war entirely at his own discretion. After all, as his spokesmen tirelessly reiterate, he is the commander in chief of the armed forces (as if this fact simply wiped out the rest of the Constitution).

Congress has become so pusillanimous that it provides no check whatever on the president's war making. In "authorizing" the presi-dent to attack Iraq or not, entirely as he pleased, Congress not only abrogated its clear constitutional duty, but it did so with grotesquely cavalier disregard for the gravity of the matter at stake. It did not even bother to debate the issue, but simply handed over its power to the executive and returned to the workaday plundering that is its only remaining raison d'etre. The president and his chief underlings keep telling us that "we are at war," but it's just a turn of phrase for public-relations purposes, inasmuch as the constitutional require-ment of a congressional declaration of war has gone unfulfilled. It provokes no great public outcry, however, so conditioned have the people become to this form of executive usurpation.

To the injury of all past attenuations of our rights under the Con-stitution, the government has now added the insult of shredding the Fourth, Fifth, and Sixth Amendments. Our rulers declare that by nothing more substantial than the emperor's say-so, any person may be arrested and held incommunicado, without trial, and then pun-ished, even put to death. Say good-bye to the writ of habeas corpus, the very bedrock of limited government. Speedy trial? Forget about it. The government has to but whisper those two magic words, *un-lawful combatant,* and you may be rendered as much a *desaparecido* as any unfortunate victim of Argentine tyranny. Surely this sort of "de-fense of our freedom" falls under the rubric of destroying the village in order to save it. As for due process of law, it's obsolete. Your right to be secure "against unreasonable searches and seizures"? That's ancient history, too, outmoded since September 11, 2001, when, the government insists, "everything changed," including your right to be free of warrantless searches of your premises, Carnivore sweeps of your e-mail, and taps of your telephone calls.

A few things definitely did not change after 9/11, however, and chief among them is the government's lust for greater power and control over every single person in the country—nay, over everyone on the entire earth. Do I fear that the USA PATRIOT Act will be abused? No. I *know* that it has been already and will continue to be as its elastic language allows unscrupulous prosecutors to scratch a variety of itches completely unrelated to terrorism. Apart from these egregious and wholly predictable prosecutorial shenanigans, freedom-loving people ought to recognize that—to borrow a phrase from Edmund Burke—the thing itself is an abuse, because it sweeps away fundamental due-process protections of our rights that required centuries to put in place.

In the face of all this and too much else even to mention, some people, even some self-described libertarians, persist in arguing that the price we are paying is worthwhile and that we can trust the government to act responsibly and effectively in wielding its new powers. Neither element of that argument will bear scrutiny.

As for trusting the government, the fact, well established in history and in contemporary reality, is that, contrary to what conservatives all seem to believe, the government can be trusted to do the right thing and to do it well even less in foreign and defense policy than it can be trusted in matters of domestic policy. Because national-security matters lie outside the immediate experience of the great bulk of the citizens, the government can get away with waste, fraud, brutality, and idiocy far more easily in foreign affairs than it can when prescribing student exams, building houses for poor people, or relieving Grandma's aches and pains. The history of U.S. foreign and defense policy in the past sixty years is an unrelieved tale of mendacity, corruption, and criminal blundering. If the government can't fix the potholes in Washington, D.C., it certainly can't build a viable liberal democratic state in Iraq. No one of sound mind could have supposed that it would even try, much less that it would succeed. This adventure, like so much else that the government undertakes, is a gigantic hoax, and all too much of it verges on racketeering of the sort described by the legendary U.S. Marine general Smedley Butler.

But if the government *were* able and willing to carry out an effective global "war on terrorism" by means of its present policy of empire and naked aggression (politely called *preventive war*), would the benefits of that policy justify the costs being borne? Not for a moment. The costs are real and huge—hundreds of billions of dollars and thousands of dead and wounded so far just for the invasion and occupation of Afghanistan and Iraq, not to mention again the grave injuries to civil and economic liberties here at home. The benefits, to the extent that any exist at all, accrue entirely to a small coterie of political leaders and their supporters among the power elite, for the most part their cronies in the military-industrial, financial, and petroleum sectors. Ideological zealots dedicated to serving the interests of Israel's Likud Party and the members of certain Christian sects thrilled by the prospect of apocalyptic mayhem in the Holy Land go along for the sheer intoxication of the spree, the former serving as high-level conspirators and disinformation specialists and the latter forming a legion of useful idiots, a sort of ten-million-strong Karl Rove Brigade on election day. Can any libertarian react except with disgust to any aspect of this criminally lethal and massively destructive government fiasco?

PART II

Airport (In)Security

Federal Oversight Won't Improve Airport Security

Recent proposals to "federalize" airport security run counter to the common-sense notion that local matters are best managed by local people.

Moreover, the history of federal intervention—in labor relations, health care, natural resources, occupational health and safety, and other areas—suggests that federalizing airport security would bring equally disappointing results.

Studies by the General Accounting Office and the Department of Transportation Inspector General, as well as the horrible events of September 11, show that airport security does need a major overhaul. Adopting a federal one-size-fits-all system, however, may lull Americans into a false sense of security. At best, it would be a poor way to foster innovation and accountability. Compare the U.S. Postal Service with FedEx, and you'll see why.

NO INCENTIVE

Simply put, federal administrators lack the incentive to do a good job. If a local airport-security manager fails, everyone knows whom to hold accountable. If a federal administrator should fail in one or two major cases, in contrast, he can always claim to have done a good job because "the system worked for 99 percent of airports."

Responsibility for airport security has been haphazardly divided among various parties—local law enforcement, the airlines, the airports, and the Federal Aviation Administration—resulting in poor accountability.

The Federal Bureau of Investigation, the Central Intelligence Agency, and the Bureau of Alcohol, Tobacco, and Firearms have

Originally appeared October 26, 2001

recently demonstrated appallingly poor performances and accountability. Why would a new federal airport-security agency do any better?

We need to create an institutional structure that aligns the interests of all involved in airport security, a system that will foster innovation and accountability.

Such a system can be created and operate successfully only in the private sector.

In recent years, many European airports have been privatized, resulting in improved service—including security—and accountability. That result benefits everyone. The United States should embrace such reform, not run away from it by placing all its eggs in a socialist basket.

9

The Pretense of Airport Security

College student Nathaniel Heatwole's recent, highly publicized hijinks in deliberately and successfully flouting airline-security rules illustrate once more the realities of the government's sham program to protect the commercial airline industry from terrorists.

The Transportation Security Administration (TSA) is a joke, and not a funny one, either. As you pass through the TSA's airport checkpoints, you can expect to overhear mutters about the "Gestapo," the "morons," and similar commentary from outraged but powerless travelers who have chosen to swallow their self-respect and submit to pointless, degrading invasions of their persons and property in order to avoid offending the thugs who, whenever they choose, can prevent passengers from proceeding with their travel. Something is horribly wrong with a population willing to tolerate such routine degradation and thuggery, especially when the alleged benefits of the humiliation are entirely bogus.

Deputy TSA administrator Stephen McHale, behaving as a bureaucrat is bound to behave, dismissed the significance of the Heatwole incident. "Amateur testing of our systems do [*sic*] not show us in any way our flaws," he said. "We know where the vulnerabilities are and we are testing them. . . . This does not help."

Well, yes, it does not help to improve a bureaucrat's day when a college student carries out with such ease multiple evasions of forbidden-item interdiction, immediately alerts the authorities to every detail of his actions, then has to wait a month for an official reaction. McHale's dismissal notwithstanding, this incident does highlight flaws that have been disclosed repeatedly by others, including agents of the Transportation Department's inspector general, ever since the

Originally appeared October 23, 2003

feds rushed to nationalize airport security screening in the wake of 9/11.

Back then, when President Bush signed the takeover bill into law on November 19, 2001, he declared: "Safety comes first. And when it comes to safety, we will set high standards and enforce them." The president was just blowing political hot air. Everybody knows that services are almost always performed worse by government employees than by private employees. Airport security screening has been no exception, as the government's own inspectors have shown again and again. A TSA survey of thirty-two major airports, reported in July 2002, for example, "found that fake guns, bombs, and other weapons got past security screeners almost one-fourth of the time."

Do not suppose, however, that the TSA has served no purpose. Primarily, it has served to give the public the impression that the government is "doing something" about airline security. The government is doing a great deal, to be sure; it's just not doing anything that contributes to genuine security. Anyone who spends half an hour thinking about how to commandeer or blow up an airplane can easily come up with a workable plan. Do we really suppose that the people smart enough to have pulled off the coordinated hijackings and attacks of 9/11 are too stupid to beat the present system?

The TSA has also served to bulk up the government payroll and, in the process, the ranks of rock-solid Democratic voters. Count this payoff to Democrats as one of the many that President Bush has been willing to make to secure Democratic votes in Congress for measures he himself ranks highly, such as running up the Pentagon's budget and attacking Iraq. Late in 2001, the airline screening industry employed some twenty-eight thousand workers. President Bush's request for fiscal year 2004 calls for the TSA to employ fifty-nine thousand, at a cost of $4.812 billion. That sum works out to $81,560 per employee. Does anyone really believe we're getting our money's worth?

Of course, we have to take into account that not all the money goes for payroll. Indeed, much of the spending ends up in the pockets of private contractors—Boeing, Lockheed Martin, Raytheon, Oracle, Unisys, InVision Technologies, and others—who have found the provision of hardware, software, training, and other services to be a godsend. Along the way, the TSA has approved at least eighty contracts worth some $54 million without normal competitive bidding. Obviously, the good-old-boy fraternity so familiar in Pentagon contracting—officially described here as "firms that TSA officials identified as having expertise in the areas needed"—has had no trouble entering the TSA's vault and walking out with cash.

Like any federal bureaucracy, the TSA has spawned its share of scandals. A widely reported one involved its booking of the Wyndham Peaks Resort and Golden Door Spa near Telluride, Colorado, to conduct recruiting interviews. Twenty TSA recruiters stayed seven weeks at this plush resort to fill fifty screener jobs. While there, they also shelled out $29,000 of the taxpayers' money to the local police department for extra security. Another scandal involved some $400,000 spent to redecorate in appropriate bureaucratic splendor the office of then-chief John Magaw (who was later fired).

When the feds were gearing up to take over the screening industry, proponents of this harebrained idea emphasized the advantages of switching from ill-trained, low-paid private employees to better-trained, higher-paid federal employees, all subjected to proper background checks. In June 2003, however, "the TSA acknowledged firing more than twelve hundred airport screeners—roughly 2 percent of its screener workforce—for providing false information on job applications, failing drug tests or having criminal records." Recently a flap broke out when it came to light that TSA employees taking certification tests had been given the exact questions and answers in advance. Evidently, these crack federal employees, who were supposed to be such tremendous improvements (though the TSA had quickly waived its initial high-school-graduation requirement), needed a slight edge to demonstrate their superiority.

TSA head Admiral James Loy affirms that although he has ordered a "full investigation," he retains "full confidence" in the agency's fifty-six thousand screeners. Evidently Admiral Loy does not fly commercial. If he had seen what the rest of us see each time we encounter this overpaid-at-any-price corps of petty tyrants, he would know better.

In what may rank as the greatest public understatement of recent times, Oregon congressman Peter DeFazio observed about the TSA screening program, "I have extraordinary concerns that we are doing something that lacks common sense." The congressman should know as well as anyone, however, that although it may lack common sense, it expresses plenty of political sense—in fact, nothing but political sense, with the usual full measure of pandering to an ignorant electorate and doling out of loot to political cronies.

In its screening program, the TSA also complies fully with political correctness, preferring to strip-search Grandma and to hassle young mothers laden with infants and their paraphernalia rather than to commit the unforgivable sin—namely, "profiling" the sort of people, the only known sort, who conceivably might be planning to hijack or blow up an airplane. Simultaneously, in further compliance with political correctness, the TSA has done everything in its power to cripple the program that Congress forced on it to train pilots to carry guns in the cockpit—one of the few measures that actually packs some antiterrorist punch, and a cheap, sensible one at that.

Ultimately, however, the TSA's program serves one political purpose above all others. It routinely abases and humiliates the entire population, rendering us docile and compliant and thereby preparing us to play our assigned role in the Police State that the Bush administration has been building relentlessly. For Attorney General Ashcroft, the federal prosecutors, and the thousands of bully boys at the Federal Bureau of Investigation, the Bureau of Alcohol, Tobacco, and Firearms, and all the other similar bureaus, nothing could be finer than a system whereby the entire population without exception is treated as suspected criminals and made to feel like inmates in a concentration camp.

PART III

The Draft

10

Will the Draft Rise from the Dead?

Nothing works as well as a crisis, real or perceived, for bringing discredited, seemingly moribund ideas back to life. A case in point is Charles Moskos and Paul Glastris's plea (*Washington Post,* November 4, 2001) for reinstatement of the draft. Not the old draft, of course, but one tailored to our current "new kind of war."

Moskos and Glastris assert that the draft should be revived because during the war on terrorism more people will be needed to perform dull, security-related jobs, and not enough people will volunteer for such employment. How do Moskos and Glastris know that ordinary incentives, such as improved pay and benefits, would fail to bring forth the requisite workers? Well, they don't know, of course, but they have no interest in finding out, either.

Their not-so-hidden agenda becomes clear enough in their remarks about the virtues of the draft in "unifying the country," about participation in "our shared national fate," and about bringing Ivy Leaguers shoulder to shoulder with less-privileged youths. Social leveling, it would appear, ranks so high that it trumps mere human liberty.

In a backhanded recognition of the desire of contemporary Americans for "choice," Moskos and Glastris propose to satisfy that desire by recommending a three-part draft in which the young men conscripted would choose among the military, homeland-security jobs, and a civilian national-service program. Some choice.

Moskos and Glastris's proposal raises several important questions, none of which they see fit to consider. Perhaps in a follow-up article they will tell us: Whatever happened to the idea that every person, even a young man, has inalienable rights to life, liberty, and the pursuit of happiness? Whatever happened to the idea that a just government is instituted to secure these rights, not to crush them underfoot upon the earliest pretext? What exactly do we gain if we can defend ourselves only by destroying the very heart and soul of what it is about this country that deserves defending?

11 | Censored Mail

Robert Higgs's Unpublished Letter to the Wall Street Journal

To the Editor, the *Wall Street Journal:*

Charles Moskos frets that owing to a diminished public tolerance for casualties, U.S. leaders "might put casualty avoidance over mission accomplishment," and he avers that only "when the privileged classes perform military service does the country define the cause as worth young people's blood" ("Our Will to Fight Depends on Who Is Willing to Die," March 20). By this curious argument, Moskos once again expresses his yearning for a wide-reaching national conscription of young men for military service.

The social levelers remain, it seems, a bloody-minded lot. They disdain a reasoned judgment of whether we the people—separate and apart from those "national leaders" Moskos seems all too ready to follow—have a genuinely vital interest in going to war. So long as the slaughter drags all classes into its maw, it is in his view ipso facto worthwhile.

Those who find Moskos's argument appealing need to be reminded that the ideal on which this country was founded was not a craving for self-sacrifice to the state or a willingness to be conscripted for any and all foreign military adventures, but a desire to enforce everyone's—even young men's—rights to life, liberty, and the pursuit of happiness. Policies that fail to respect that great ideal should be opposed, and conscription stands high among the proposals that cry out for a free people's opposition.

Originally appeared April 2, 2002

PART IV

The Political Economy of the Military-Industrial-Congressional Complex

12

The Cold War

Too Good a Deal to Give Up

For years, Pentagon watchers have remarked on the curious fact that the end of the Cold War failed to bring about a substantive change in the care and feeding of the U.S. military establishment. Yes, the "defense and international" budget did fall from its Gulf War height of $314.5 billion in fiscal year 1992, and it failed to keep up with the growth of the economy, dropping to 3.2 percent of gross domestic product by the late 1990s. Still, considering that the United States no longer faced any powerful enemy comparable to the once-mighty USSR, some observers considered it odd that in inflation-adjusted terms, the military budget during the six fiscal years from 1995 through 2000 was equal to what it had been during the baseline years (1955–65 and 1974–80) of the Cold War. Moreover, the Pentagon continued to spend its money for the same kinds of forces and weapons that had been developed specifically for confrontations with the Red Army or a similar foe. Times had changed, but the generals hadn't.

I was among those making such observations. Early in 2001, I composed an article called "The Cold War Is Over, but U.S. Preparation for It Continues" for the fall issue of the *Independent Review.* As fate would have it, this issue was passing through the mail to subscribers when the terrorist attacks of September 11 took place. In the article, I had observed that the U.S. military establishment was not being managed so as to provide security against terrorist attacks on Americans at home—a remark that, to some readers, later seemed prophetic—but I had scarcely been a lone voice crying out in the wilderness. Others had been warning for years of precisely the same misallocation of defense resources.

Originally appeared February 27, 2002

The Hart-Rudman Commission, for example, had highlighted the threat of international terrorism, noting that Americans no longer enjoy a "relative invulnerability of the U.S. homeland to catastrophic attack" and predicting that "[a] direct attack against American citizens on American soil is likely over the next quarter century." The Department of Defense, the commission concluded, "appears incapable of generating a strategic posture very different from that of the Cold War, and its weapons acquisition process is slow, inefficient, and burdened by excess regulation." Declaring that the Department of Defense "needs to pay far more attention to this [homeland defense] mission in the future," the commission recommended that "a new office of Assistant Secretary for Homeland Security be created to oversee DoD activities in this domain and to ensure that the necessary resources are made available." Such reports, one comes to expect, are duly noted by the press and then pass into obscurity more or less ignored by the busy people who populate the military-industrial-congressional complex (hereafter, the MICC), and this particular report was no exception.

Shortly after the September 11 attacks, President Bush did move in the direction recommended by the Hart-Rudman Commission when he created the Office of Homeland Security. One wonders how many Americans have stopped to ponder the meaning of that action? For more than fifty years, the United States has maintained an active—some might say hyperactive—Department of Defense. If it does not defend our homeland, what does it defend?

Whatever the answer might be, the Pentagon has not been shy about spending our money. During the more than forty years of Cold War, annual military spending averaged 7.5 percent of gross national product, and just in the past five years military spending has cumulated to more than $1.5 trillion. You'd think that so much money would purchase a lot of national security. Yet, apart from the catastrophic attack on New York City, the defense establishment, along with its numerous in-house and affiliated "intelligence" organizations, failed even to anticipate or to defend against the devastating attack on its own headquarters.

On October 1, 2001, the Pentagon issued its *Quadrennial Defense Review.* As *New York Times* reporter Thom Shanker noted, this review "restores the defense of the United States as the department's primary mission." One can't help wondering: What was its primary mission before? Would you believe these imperial objectives: stationing forces worldwide, propping up allied governments, deterring threats to U.S. interests abroad, and, should the need arise, fighting a couple of those ever-popular foreign wars?

On October 23, 2001, the Defense Department issued an announcement seeking contract proposals for "combating terrorism, location and defeat of hard or difficult targets, protracted operations in remote areas, and countermeasures to weapons of mass destruction." It seems the Pentagon is—now—in a hurry in its counterterrorism efforts because it seeks "near-term solutions" to be developed in twelve to eighteen months. You don't need to be a defense specialist to see that the Pentagon was caught off-guard by the recent attacks on the United States, by the manner in which they were carried out, and by the nature of the perpetrators. So you have to wonder: What were all those defense bigwigs doing with all that money during the past decade?

Well, as anyone who bothered to look would have noticed, they were continuing to fight the Cold War, even though that conflict had ended in the early 1990s with the disintegration of the Soviet Union. Notwithstanding the evaporation of the once-formidable Red Army, the lion's share of recent defense spending has gone—and continues to go—toward maintaining a force equipped with Cold War weapons—high-tech combat aircraft, warships, missiles, satellites, and so forth. A politically entrenched defense industry makes sure that such spending continues at a high level, and pork-dispensing congressmen grease the wheels, buying a few votes in the process.

Even though the September 11 attackers launched their mission with decidedly low-tech weapons—box cutters—the MICC, in defiance of all logic, has redoubled its efforts to milk the established high-tech cash cows. For example, Northrup-Grumman and its friends in high places now perceive an opportunity to resume production of the quintessential Cold War weapons platform, the B-2 bomber, at a cost of some $28 billion for gearing up the assembly line and turning out another forty aircraft. In the view of Congressman Duncan Hunter (R-Calif.), chairman of the House Armed Services Committee's subcommittee on research and development, the war on terrorism has shown that "long-range and precision-strike capabilities are going to be even more valuable than before." Yeah, sure.

According to the *Wall Street Journal,* "the F-22 and nearly every other expensive Pentagon weapon suddenly has become immune to major budget cuts" since the terrorists commandeered the four airliners in September. For the Defense Department and its contractors, "that means keeping every current big-ticket item and adding a few new ones." In the immortal words of Boeing vice chairman Harry Stonecipher, "the purse is now open," and members of Congress who oppose the new spending frenzy by arguing that "we don't have the resources to defend America . . . won't be there after November" 2002. Bizarrely, even the granddaddy of all military boondoggles, the ballistic-missile-defense system, has regained its momentum in the aftermath of the terrorists' use of nonballistic missiles conveniently made available by United Airlines and American Airlines.

As Independent Institute defense analyst Ivan Eland (director, Center on Peace & Liberty) has recently remarked of the Bush administration's proposal to increase defense spending by $48 billion, or 12 percent, during the fiscal year 2003, "Most of the defense budget increase has little to do with winning the war on terrorism." Just as the Korean War once served as the pretext for vastly increasing military spending on weapons and forces positioned worldwide, the so-called war on terrorism now serves as the pretext for throwing money at every constituent in the MICC. The *Wall Street Journal* confirms, "The antiterror campaign is making for some remarkably flush times for the military, and the need for hard choices on weapons systems has all but evaporated." For all the big weapons systems and all the big contractors, the threat of project cancellations or spending cutbacks is now a thing of the past.

Members of Congress, never satisfied until a maximum amount of the defense budget has been diverted toward buying votes for their reelection, are not objecting to the huge increase in military spending, but they want no reallocations whatsoever away from the established Cold War programs that currently channel taxpayer money to their political backers: "In a bipartisan voice," reports James Dao of the *New York Times,* "lawmakers on Capitol Hill are telling the Pentagon that they want to increase spending on conventional big-ticket weapons programs, particularly warships and planes, raising new questions about Defense Secretary Donald Rumsfeld's ability to revamp the military with newer types of technology."

And so it goes. For those with an appreciation of the past sixty years of U.S. history, it's déjà vu again. This time, however, Americans may have to pay a higher price in blood as well as money for the maintenance of their blessed MICC. The Pentagon's business-as-usual defense policy—obviously—failed to defend the American people on September 11. Nor can we expect it to defend them in the future. Just possibly, what's good for Lockheed-Martin, the top brass at the Pentagon, and the congressmen in cahoots with them is not necessarily good for national security.

13

U.S. National Security
Illusions versus Realities

For nearly all of us, U.S. "national security" involves policies and practices remote from our personal experience. What we know about this subject comes for the most part from what we see on television or read about in the newspapers. As a result, we tend to fall prey to disinformation broadcast by parties with an axe to grind. The U.S. administration is always the most important such interested party. Now more than ever, as the government prosecutes a so-called war on terrorism without a visible enemy or a definable resolution, it behooves us to separate illusions from realities.

ILLUSION NO. 1: The U.S. Defense Department protects the American people in America.

REALITY NO. 1: The Defense Department occupies itself overwhelmingly in preparing for or engaging in foreign wars against persons who do not pose serious threats to the American people in America. The proposals now being considered for the creation of a Department of Homeland Security highlight the fact that heretofore the defense and intelligence establishments have given little thought and directed few of their actions toward defending U.S. citizens on their own soil.

During the Cold War, the Defense Department prepared for wars in Europe, Asia, the Middle East, and elsewhere against the Soviet Union and its surrogates. In doing so, the U.S. military establishment routinely protected regimes that at least pretended to oppose communism—no matter how tyrannical or murderous those regimes were.

Originally appeared June 30, 2002

Since the end of the Cold War, the Defense Department has undertaken to defend certain persons—many of them none too savory—in Kuwait, Saudi Arabia, Kurdistan, and southern Iraq; in Somalia, Haiti, Bosnia, and Kosovo; as well as the usual suspects in western Europe, Japan, South Korea, and Taiwan. Very little of this activity has had a direct connection with actually protecting the American people in America, and much of it has had no genuine connection whatsoever.

ILLUSION NO. 2: The Defense Department has the motivation and the capacity to manage effectively the vast resources placed at its disposal in a way that enhances the security of the American people in America.

REALITY NO. 2: The Defense Department is either unable or unwilling to deal seriously with its decades-long engagement in massive waste, fraud, and mismanagement, especially (but not exclusively) in its relations with the big defense-contracting companies.

The Defense Department will not even obey the laws with regard to its own accounting practices. According to a report by the department's inspector general, dated February 15, 2001:

> We identified $1.1 trillion in department-level accounting entries to financial data used to prepare DoD component financial statements that were not supported by adequate audit trails or by sufficient evidence to determine their validity. In addition, we also identified $107 billion in department-level accounting entries to financial data used to prepare DoD component financial statements that were improper because the entries were illogical or did not follow accounting principles. . . . [Further,] DoD did not fully comply with the laws and regulations that had a direct and material effect on its ability to determine financial statement amounts.

The government's audit agencies also found the accounts of the individual armed services in a mess, so that those records could not be audited. According to the memorandum previously cited, "The

Military Department audit agencies attempted to audit those financial statements and issued disclaimers of opinion." However, the Department of Defense inspector general did report that "[t]he financial data reported on the FY 2000 financial statements for Army, Navy, and Air Force General Funds; the Army, Navy, and Air Force Working Capital Funds; and the U.S. Army Corps of Engineers, Civil Works Program, were unauditable and comprise a significant portion of the financial data reported on the DoD Agency-wide Financial Statements for FY 2000."

And to think: Congress is wasting time holding hearings on the accounting shortcomings of Arthur Andersen and Enron, and the president is threatening to sic the Department of Justice on accounting malefactors such as WorldCom and Xerox—all of which are veritable paragons of accounting probity by comparison with the Pentagon. (Of course, various parties benefit from this blatant lawlessness and public irresponsibility. In this brief article, I cannot take up the important question of cui bono, but some of the beneficiaries are no doubt sufficiently obvious.)

ILLUSION NO. 3: Since September 11, everything is different.

REALITY NO. 3: Very little of any significance has changed in the allocation of funds and the managerial conduct of the U.S. military and intelligence apparatus since September 11. The most notable change is that the Bush administration and Congress have seen fit to give vast additional amounts of taxpayer money—amounts projected to increase annual military spending by some $120 billion in the next five years—amounts that, in large part, are certain to be wasted in the usual fashion.

Defense Secretary Donald Rumsfeld himself testified to Congress last year: "We have an obligation to taxpayers to spend their money wisely. Today, we're not doing that." Rumsfeld's statement merits an award for understatement because anyone who has spent even a little time looking into the matter knows that the Defense

Department has been wasting the taxpayers' money by the shipload, year in and year out, for decades. Nor is any improvement in sight. On the contrary, the new infusions of funds will only encourage greater waste and abuse.

The destruction of the World Trade Center—not to speak of the damage to the Pentagon itself—will remain forever an indictment of the failure of U.S. defense and intelligence policy and practice. The most curious upshot of this terrible failure is that the president and Congress have not seen fit to punish those responsible for the failure—no heads have rolled; hell, nobody has even had his wrists slapped. Instead, the failed defense and intelligence establishment is now being rewarded with the greatest infusion of new taxpayer money it has absorbed in a generation.

14

The Government Needs to Get Its Own Accounting House in Order

President Bush has been lashing out at corporate accounting shenanigans. "Corporate America has got to understand," he declares, "there's a higher calling than trying to fudge the numbers, trying to slip a billion here or a billion there and maybe hope nobody notices." In the wake of scandals at Enron, WorldCom, Xerox, and other big companies, the president warns that the Justice Department will prosecute corporations that play fast and loose with their accounts.

The Democrats, smelling blood in the water, are trying to tie the Bush administration to the accounting miscreants. Senate leader Tom Daschle blames "a deregulatory, permissive atmosphere that has relied too much on corporate America to police itself," and he points specifically to problems at Halliburton, which Vice President Dick Cheney headed not long ago. The Republicans' "laissez-faire attitude," Daschle claims, has encouraged the corporate titans to lie, cheat, and steal.

What nobody seems to notice is that while Enron, WorldCom, and the other corporate bad boys are getting their comeuppance in the stock market and sink into bankruptcy, the biggest accounting scofflaw of all continues merrily along its irresponsible way. I refer to none other than the organization with which both Bush and Daschle are connected, the federal government. Whereas Enron and WorldCom have misbehaved with billions of dollars in bad accounts, the federal government has misbehaved—and continues to misbehave, contrary to a number of federal statutes—with trillions of dollars in bad accounts.

Originally appeared July 9, 2002

Although by no means the only guilty agency, the Department of Defense is by far the worst offender. Since 1994, federal law has required government departments to make financial audits. Seems reasonable, given the trillions of dollars of taxpayer money that pass through the bureaucrats' hands each year. The Defense Department, however, has never been able to comply with the auditing requirement because its records are such a mess that they cannot even be audited.

A memorandum of February 15, 2001, signed by David K. Steensma, deputy assistant inspector general for auditing, states that "[the] DoD could not provide sufficient or reliable information for us to evaluate management's assertions or verify amounts on the FY 2000 DoD Agency-wide Financial Statements."

Moreover, "We identified $1.1 trillion in department-level accounting entries to financial data used to prepare DoD component financial statements that were not supported by adequate audit trails or by sufficient evidence to determine their validity. In addition, we also identified $107 billion in department-level accounting entries to financial data used to prepare DoD component financial statements that were improper because the entries were illogical or did not follow accounting principles."

The preceding assessment applies only to departmentwide accounting problems. The auditors also found the accounts for the individual military services to be a complete mess.

The Department of Defense has broken the law year after year. According to the Steensma memorandum, "DoD did not fully comply with the laws and regulations that had a direct and material effect on its ability to determine financial statement amounts. DoD financial management systems were not in substantial compliance with Federal financial management system requirements; applicable Federal accounting standards; and the U.S. Government Standard General Ledger at the transaction level, as required by the Federal Financial Management Improvement Act of 1996."

Last year, Defense Secretary Donald Rumsfeld told Congress,

"We have an obligation to taxpayers to spend their money wisely. Today, we're not doing that."

Talk about an understatement. Not only is the Department of Defense wasting money by the shipload, but it hasn't the foggiest idea of how many trillions of dollars it has squandered and how it has done so over the past decade. Yet department officials also have testified that no compliance with the law is in sight. The Pentagon lawbreakers simply expect to go on breaking the law and to get away with it as they have been getting away with it for years.

In a letter to Rumsfeld dated April 27, 2001, Congressmen Christopher Shays and Dennis Kucinich stated, "The Department of Defense Inspector General testified before Congress in 1995 that a turnaround in the Pentagon's budgeting practices might be expected by the year 2000. Hundreds of auditors and tens of billions of dollars in recommended adjustments later, DoD's books remain in shambles. To date, *no major part of the Department of Defense has been able to pass the test of an independent audit*" (emphasis in original).

When Enron or WorldCom can't present a proper audit statement, they are ruined. When the Department of Defense cannot put its financial records in shape even to be audited, the department is rewarded with the biggest increase in its budget since Ronald Reagan's first term as president.

15 | Nation Trembles as Congress Reassembles

The gang that Mark Twain called "America's only native criminal class" has returned to Washington. Get ready for a lot of bad news. So long as Congress remains in session, everyone's life, liberty, and property will be in heightened jeopardy.

In a government of divided powers, our national legislature is the most craven and irresponsible branch. Congress attracts a special breed of men and women. They are ambitious to get and to keep their offices. They are willing to do almost anything, so long as it is dishonorable, to remain in their positions. Think of Congress as a glorified brothel, and ask yourself what kind of people work in a brothel. When they are not out hustling money for their campaign funds, they are dreaming up ways to claim credit they do not deserve and to shift the blame they do deserve.

In any event, they're back at work now, and they've a lot to do. Well, actually, they have only one thing to do; they always have just one thing to do, and that's to get themselves reelected. The next election will take place on November 5, so there's not much time left for these harlots to do what they do best. Look for them to work overtime.

For the next two months, we'll all be bombarded by salvos of TV advertising paid for by the people who give money to the members of Congress so that after those members have been reelected, they'll give the taxpayers' money to their supporters, who will realize a 10,000 percent rate of return on their investment. These TV ads will show Congressman Smedley, smiling like a freshly painted clown, standing arm in arm with the handsome Mrs. Smedley and the couple's four well-scrubbed teenage brats, all of whom will be flashing the same wholesome, toothy, moronic smiles. What a fine family they must be! Against a background consisting of a gently waving U.S. flag and a patriotic sound track, the message will be thrust at the viewer: vote for Smedley; his scumbag opponent would screw you even worse.

Meanwhile, these worthy public servants have to keep themselves busy in Washington for a few weeks before they can evacuate the D.C. swamps and rush back to Peoria to embrace the geezers in nursing homes and to kiss ass in corporate offices and union halls. In particular, they must occupy themselves now in drawing up plans for a gigantic new federal bureau, the Department of Homeland Security (DHS). It won't be easy, so don't be surprised if they don't get it done before the election.

The problem, you see, is that Congress divides its "business" into a multitude of fiefdoms ruled by committee chairmen and chairmadams. In each area, these robber barons hold nearly all the power in their grubby hands. Because Congress divides the power in this way, the interest groups that want to feast at taxpayer expense have to get past the relevant barons first, and for that privilege they must pay. Congress is nothing if not an organization built on the principle of quid pro quo.

Right now, congressional oversight of the more than twenty agencies slated to be combined in the new DHS is divided, according to a White House count, among eighty-eight committees and subcommittees. Spending for the new agency's component parts now gains its approval from ten of the thirteen appropriations subcommittees. So a great many members of Congress now possess a valuable piece of the action. Do you think they are eager to give up the very powers they wield to extract dough and deference from petitioners who seek what only they can give? Not bloody likely. Already, more than fifty hearings have taken place on homeland-security matters.

To make matters even more complicated, President Bush is insisting that he be given authority to hire, fire, and set pay rates for the estimated 170,000 employees of the new department, thereby robbing the barons of their patronage and cutting into the power of the public-employee unions. Senator Joseph Lieberman has let it be known that the president is asking much too much, and Senator Robert Byrd, the evil procedural genius of the upper house, is pawing the earth and expressing grave reservations about the administration's DHS proposal.

Besides the DHS job, which probably won't get done on time, Congress intends to explore how much damage it can do by monkeying with employee-pension arrangements, a terrorism-insurance subsidy, a massive prescription-drug giveaway, and federal aid to so-called faith-based providers of government largess. You want to talk about something faith-based, then talk about the beliefs of people who suppose that anything good can come out of Congress's fiddling with such matters. Why not be honest and call the postelection session that looms not the lame-duck session but the lamebrain session.

All this, of course, is but democracy in action, so eat it up, all you democrats. But if you are going to select representatives to the ruling crowd by means of what H. L. Mencken called "advance auctions of stolen goods," don't be surprised if you wake up and find yourself subject to people who make ordinary pickpockets look, by comparison, nearly noble.

16 | If We're Really in Danger, Why Doesn't the Government Act as if We're in Danger?

President George W. Bush, Vice President Dick Cheney, Defense Secretary Donald Rumsfeld, Homeland Security Adviser Tom Ridge, and other government leaders rarely miss an opportunity nowadays to remind us of the grave danger we face. In a speech on July 16, the president declared, "We are today a nation at risk to a new and changing threat." Noting that "the terrorist threat to America takes many forms, has many places to hide, and is often invisible," the president emphasized "our enduring vulnerability." Evidently, the danger has not diminished much lately. I have just checked the threat indicator at the Web site of the Office of Homeland Security and found it, as of October 27, to be yellow, signifying an "elevated" level.

Obviously, we're in a world of trouble. Equally obviously, the government accepts full responsibility for allaying the threat its leaders say we face. As the president himself put it in the July 16 speech, "The U.S. government has no more important mission than protecting the homeland from future terrorist attack."

But you've got to wonder. If we are really in such danger, why doesn't the government act as if we are? Danger is supposed to focus the mind and sharpen one's responses. The actions of the federal government, however, continue to be anything but focused. "Scattered to hell and back" describes them more accurately.

Consider, for example, that not long ago Congress passed and the president signed a farm bill that will increase spending by some $83 billion over the next decade. All disinterested parties recognize that the greater part of this vast sum constitutes nothing but welfare for rich landowners and related agribusiness interests. Regardless of how we might characterize it, however, one thing's for sure: every dollar spent on agricultural subsidies is a dollar not spent on fighting terrorism. If terrorists menace us so seriously, why is the government squandering precious fiscal resources on welfare for agribusiness?

Even a small portion of the money being shoveled to farmers would go a long way toward modernizing the FBI's outdated computer system—you know, the one that couldn't collate and communicate all the information the government possessed about the men who later hijacked the airliners on September 11, 2001. The FBI now claims that it will invest in new computers and that it will add some nine hundred agents to its payroll, some of them actually knowledgeable in foreign languages (some Arabic speakers might be nice for a change), but the bureau continues to complain that it is hard pressed for budgetary resources.

Rather than financing still another wing on Farmer Smith's rural palace, why not use some of the farm loot to buy information about what the terrorists are plotting in their various haunts around the world? Just $10 billion of the agrisubsidy money—mere chump change for the Farm Bureau guys—would go a long, long way in loosening the tongues of informants in the back alleys of Karachi, Lahore, and Kuala Lumpur. That information might help to save American lives, which is a bit more than you can say for doling out megabillions to the rice, corn, and cotton kings of this country.

The farm program, however, is scarcely the sole example of the government's misshapen conduct. Evidently it hasn't occurred to anybody in the government that the agencies responsible for dealing with the terrorist threat might need the public's money more than, say, the federal education and training programs, which have been soaking up more than $40 billion annually—and I need not remind the reader just how effective those dollars have been in raising the reading, writing, and arithmetic skills of the student population. Or maybe we could reallocate some of the $11 billion dished out each year for "community and regional development." Isn't it more pressing to obstruct the next gang of mad bombers than to fund more bike paths?

The entire Justice Department, which includes the FBI and other agencies assigned to preventing terrorism, employs some 126,000 persons (reported at the end of fiscal year 2000). Why can't the government bulk up its corps of critical protective workers by cutting away some of the 104,000 employees of the Department of Agriculture (or, barring that possibility, by diverting some of the G-men from the cruel and futile drug war)? Pretty soon the Agriculture Department's staff will exceed the number of full-time farmers in the country. Shouldn't a nation truly threatened with mortal danger try to deal with that danger rather than spend its resources on still another study of fluctuations in the yield of kumquats?

On October 23, the president signed into law the Defense Department's appropriation act for fiscal year 2003. It provides the Pentagon with $355 billion, a whopping 12 percent more than last year's budget. The military construction bill provides an additional $10.5 billion; the Energy Department bill will add some $15 billion for the military's nuclear-weapons programs; and eventually Congress will cough up another $10 billion for a "contingency" account the president wants to use as a military slush fund.

Lest you think that this huge pot of money bears some relation to the fight against terrorism, you ought to consider the specific accounts it funds, such as $7.4 billion for the budgetary black hole known as ballistic missile defense; $1.5 billion for another Virginia-class attack submarine to use against the nearly nonexistent Russian navy; $4.7 billion for research and development on the F-22, plus twenty-three of the actual high-performance fighters, to use against the nearly nonexistent Russian air force; $1.6 billion for eleven V-22 Osprey tilt-rotor aircraft, a contraption so ill-designed that it poses a greater threat to its occupants than to any enemy; and $3.2 billion for forty-six more F/A-18E/F fighters, to maintain air superiority over—well, they'll think of somebody.

"Our enemy," George W. Bush has said, "is smart and resolute."

All right, maybe so. But the president has insisted, "We are smarter and more resolute." Unfortunately, this claim does not sit comfortably with the facts. A smarter and more resolute government would not throw away the resources needed to ward off terrorists, using the available funds instead to finance winter vacations in Martinique for wealthy farmers or to bankroll still another eminently dispensable "community-development" project, or to keep a hundred thousand otiose employees on the payroll at the Department of Agriculture. A smarter and more resolute government would not fritter away scores of billions of dollars annually on producing, deploying, and maintaining an array of weapon systems fit only for fighting a USSR that no longer exists.

It is all too clear that either we are not really in grave danger, and hence the government's actions, though sufficiently objectionable in many ways, are not lethally reprehensible, or we really are in grave danger and, given that condition, the government is acting in a completely irresponsible and utterly immoral manner. If semi-organized gangs of suicidal maniacs numbering in the thousands are out to kill us all, the government ought not to be fiddling with kindergarten subsidies and the preservation of the slightly spotted southeastern screech owl. It ought to get serious.

Early in the twentieth century, a colorful character by the name of Smedley D. Butler rose to the rank of major general in the U.S. Marine Corps, serving in many places around the world and twice being awarded the Congressional Metal of Honor. In 1935, in retirement, he wrote a tract titled "War Is a Racket," in which he drew on his personal experiences to explain how some people—politicians, bankers, and munitions makers—profit from war, while other people—ordinary soldiers and taxpayers—bear the costs of war in blood and treasure. War is not what it's cracked up to be by those who lead the nation into it, he argued. It's just a racket.

Butler had in mind U.S. participation in World War I as well as U.S. interventions in Asia, Latin America, and the Caribbean. He died in 1940, so he never witnessed the even wider-ranging global interventionism in which the United States has engaged during the past sixty years. If he were alive today, however, I have no doubt about how he would perceive the government's so-called war on terrorism. I even have a hunch about the word he would use to describe it.

17

Free Enterprise and War, a Dangerous Liaison

Some prominent pro-market think tanks are promoting more than free enterprise these days. They're also peddling war. Among the American Enterprise Institute's (AEI) recent offerings, for example, is a forthrightly bellicose bulletin written by AEI resident fellow Reuel Marc Gerecht entitled "A Necessary War." Although I do not find Gerecht's arguments in favor of a U.S. military conquest of Iraq to be compelling, my purpose here is not to comment on the essay itself, but rather to make some observations about the more general phenomenon that its issuance exemplifies—namely, the death wish expressed in the postwar conservative embrace of free enterprise and the warfare state.

Ever since the demise of the Taft wing of the Republican Party in the early 1950s, U.S. conservatives with few exceptions have believed and acted on the belief that we can have free enterprise and a warfare state at the same time. They have been mistaken.

The sprawling, voracious, military-industrial complex has constituted anything but free enterprise from its very inception during World War II. In this vast cesspool of mismanagement, waste, and transgressions not only bordering on but often entering deeply into criminal conduct, no consumer-determined bottom line has dictated which firms would survive and which would go bankrupt. Instead, recurrent government bailouts have been the order of the day. The great arms firms have managed to slough off much of the normal risk of doing business in a genuine market, passing on many of their excessive costs to the taxpayers while still realizing extraordinary rates of return on investment. Meanwhile, high taxes to support the military-industrial complex have punished all those striving to operate businesses in the actual free market.

Nor has this economic mess been the worst aspect of the operation of the military contracting business. Far more malign has been the role these semisocialized firms have played as powerful insiders in the making of strategic and foreign policy, constantly exerting strong direct and indirect pressures to maintain America's imperial posture in the world, to keep up the quick pace of the arms race, and to increase the already enormous bulk of the defense budget. Working for peace, not to speak of working for free enterprise, has never been their profession, as anyone attending their trade-association conferences or reading their advertisements in defense-industry magazines can easily attest.

Had the postwar conservatives given any thought to the effects of U.S. participation in the two world wars, they would have realized right away the futility of trying to combine free enterprise with preparation for or engagement in war.

In World War I, the government imposed a variety of unprecedented controls on businesses. It nationalized outright the firms in the railroad, telephone, and telegraph industries and, for all practical purposes, those engaged in the ocean shipping industry as well. It fixed scores of industrial commodity prices, intervened extensively in management-labor relations, and promoted unionization and collective bargaining. It hiked corporate income taxes to undreamt-of heights and added a huge excess-profits tax on top of them. The net result of all this government dictation, taxation, takeover, and all-around meddling became known to contemporaries as "war socialism."

Although the government released its grip on private enterprise after the war ended, government-business relations never returned to their prewar status. When Congress returned the railroad companies to their private owners in 1920, for example, it did so with so many strings attached that thereafter the great U.S. railroad industry became little more than a quasi public utility. Corporate tax rates were lowered, but never to their prewar levels.

The war's ideological legacies put even more pernicious pressures on the free-enterprise system. The government's economic managers, led by the chairman of the War Industries Board, Bernard Baruch, emerged from their wartime service convinced (against the bulk of the evidence) that they could and should preside over the economy even in peacetime. As one historian wrote, they "meditated with a sort of intellectual contempt on the huge hit-and-miss confusion of peace-time industry." As Baruch himself put it, "Our experience taught that government direction of the economy need not be inefficient or undemocratic, and suggested that in time of danger it was imperative."

Imbued with this ill-founded hubris, the former wartime central planners, led during the 1920s by the energetic Secretary of Commerce Herbert Hoover, undertook to "rationalize" industrial practices by fostering product standardization, the formation of trade associations, and more intimate "business-government cooperation." This quasi-cartelizing activity helped to suppress normal market competition and softened up businessmen for later acceptance of the semifascist National Industrial Recovery Act of 1933—the complete realization of the Baruch gang's ambitions and, with respect to recovery from the Great Depression, nothing short of a disaster.

During World War II, the government went even further in imposing its will on free enterprise. The wartime central planners implemented comprehensive wage and price controls, rigged interest rates, rationed credit, and capped rents. The War Production Board didn't just allocate scarce raw materials. It dictated which industries might operate and which might not—the great civilian auto industry, for example, was shut down completely for more than three years. Corporate income taxes went sky high and, again, gigantic excess-profits taxes added insult to injury. So completely did the armed forces dominate the allocation of economic resources during the war that the privately owned capital stock actually shrank because, except in the munitions industries, the owners were unable to secure enough investment funds and replacement materials to make up for normal wear and tear.

Again the government, as it had after World War I, abandoned the bulk (not all) of its wartime business controls when the war ended. Corporate income-tax rates were reduced from their wartime heights, yet they remained at extraordinarily high levels for decades afterward. The government's meddling in international economic affairs, which had assumed massive proportions during the war, persisted in the form of "foreign aid," in large part a disguised business-subsidy program that rendered the participating firms beholden to their government benefactors and left the great majority of firms sharing its costs but receiving none of its subsidies.

During the war, tens of thousands of business executives had served in the government's planning and control bureaucracy. According to contemporary economist Calvin Hoover, writing in 1959, that experience "conditioned them to accept a degree of governmental intervention and control after the war which they had deeply resented prior to it." Thus, it is scarcely surprising that even the pro-business Eisenhower administration did nothing of substance to diminish the pervasive federal government presence in the economy that had been spawned by World War I and nourished by the New Deal and that had reached its zenith during World War II.

Historically, as government has sought to extend its sway over private enterprise in the United States, only one great faction has had the power to resist effectively—namely, the business sector. But this potential defender of free enterprise had its ideological back broken twice in quick succession, during the two world wars. By the time the Cold War began in the late 1940s, businessmen had been tamed once and for all, put in their place of subservience to government masters. Resigned to making the best of a bad situation, entrepreneurs have searched for opportunities in the little spaces not yet closed off by the government's interposition. For the past half century, however, free enterprise has been at best a hobbled and heavily burdened horse. If it has continued to pull the economic load, it has done so in spite of all that government has done to cripple it, not because its effective functioning has proved congruous with the operation of the warfare state.

For conservatives who now claim to support both free enterprise and a U.S. war of conquest against Iraq, the lesson ought to be plain: they cannot foster free enterprise and support war—the greatest of all socialistic undertakings—at the same time. Unfortunately, it appears that once again they are willing to sacrifice free enterprise on the altar of Mars.

18

War Prosperity
The Fallacy that Won't Die

To the Editor, the *Wall Street Journal:*

Bob Davis and Greg Jaffe's article (*Wall Street Journal,* February 4) on the likely economic consequences of a U.S. war against Iraq errs by giving past wars credit for creating positive economic effects. This hoary fallacy, it seems, just can't be killed.

The strongest case for it has long been World War II, which Davis and Jaffe claim "clearly was a boon for the U.S. economy." But a boon in what sense? Unemployment fell during the war entirely because of the buildup of the armed forces. In 1940, some 4.62 million persons were actually unemployed (the official count of 7.45 million included 2.83 million employed on various government work projects). During the war, the government, by conscription for the most part, drew some 16 million persons into the armed forces at some time; the active-duty force in mid-1945 numbered in excess of 12 million. Voilà, civilian unemployment nearly disappeared. But herding the equivalent of 22 percent of the prewar labor force into the armed forces (to eliminate 9.5 percent unemployment) scarcely produced what we are properly entitled to call prosperity.

Yes, officially measured gross domestic product (GDP) soared during the war. Examination of that increased output shows, however, that it consisted entirely of military goods and services. Both real civilian consumption and private investment fell after 1941, and they did not recover fully until 1946. The privately owned capital stock actually shrank during the war. Some prosperity. (My article "Wartime Prosperity? A Reassessment of the U.S. Economy in the

1940s," *Journal of Economic History,* March 1992, presents many of the relevant details.)

It is high time that we come to appreciate the distinction between the government spending, especially the war spending, that bulks up official GDP figures and the kinds of production that create genuine economic prosperity. As Ludwig von Mises wrote in the aftermath of World War I, "war prosperity is like the prosperity that an earthquake or a plague brings."

19

Suppose You Wanted to Have a Permanent War

I'll concede that having a permanent war might seem an odd thing to want, but let's put aside the "why" question for the time being, accepting that you wouldn't want it unless you stood to gain something important from it. If, however, for reasons you found adequate, you did want to have a permanent war, what would you need in order to make such a policy viable in a democratic society such as the United States?

First, you would need that society to have a dominant ideology— a widely shared belief system about social and political relations— within which having a permanent war seems to be a desirable policy, given the ideology's own content and the pertinent facts accepted by its adherents. Something like American jingo-patriotism cum anti-communism might turn the trick. It worked pretty well during the nearly half century of the Cold War. The beauty of anticommunism as a covering ideology was that it could serve to justify a wide variety of politically expedient actions both here and abroad. The Commies, you'll recall, were everywhere: not just in Moscow and Sevastopol, but maybe in Minneapolis and San Francisco. We had to stay alert; we could never let down our guard, anywhere.

Second, you would need periodic crises, because without them the public becomes complaisant, unafraid, and hence unwilling to bear the heavy burdens that they must bear if the government is to carry on a permanent war. As Senator Arthur Vandenberg told Harry Truman in 1947 at the outset of the Cold War, gaining public support for a perpetual global campaign requires that the government "scare hell out of the American people." Each crisis piques the people's insecurities and renders them once again disposed to pay the designated price, whether it takes the form of their treasure, their liberties, or their young men's blood. Something like the (alleged) missile gap, the (alleged) Gulf of Tonkin attacks on U.S. naval vessels, or the (actual!) hostage taking at the U.S. embassy in Tehran will do nicely, at least for a while. Crises by their very nature eventually recede, and new ones must come along—or be made to come along—to serve the current need.

Third, you would need some politically powerful groups whose members stand to gain substantially from a permanent war in terms of achieving their urgent personal and group objectives. Call me crass, but I've noticed that few people will stay engaged for long unless there's "something in it for them."

During the Cold War, the conglomeration of personally interested parties consisted of those who form the military-industrial-congressional complex (MICC). The generals and admirals thrived by commanding a large armed force sustained by a lavish budget. The big defense contractors enjoyed ample returns at minimal risk (because they could expect that should they screw up too royally, a bailout would be forthcoming). Members of Congress who belonged to the military oversight and appropriations committees could parlay their positions into campaign contributions and various sorts of income in kind. Presiding over the entire complex, of course, the president, his National Security Council, and their many subordinates, advisers, consultants, and hangers-on enjoyed the political advantages associated with control of a great nation's diplomatic and military affairs—not to speak of the sheer joy that certain people get from wielding or influencing great power. No conspiracy here, of course, just a lot of people fitting into their niches, doing well while proclaiming that they were doing good (recall the ideology and the crisis elements). All seeking only to serve the common public interest. Absolutely.

The foregoing observations have been widely accepted by several generations of students of the Cold War. Yet, now, you may protest, the Cold War is over, the USSR nonexistent, the menace of communism kaput. Under post–Cold War conditions, how can we have a permanent war? Well, all we need to do is to replace the missing piece.

If the ideology of anticommunism can no longer serve to justify a permanent war, let us put in its place the overarching rationale of a "war on terrorism." In fact, this substitution of what President George W. Bush repeatedly calls "a new kind of war" amounts to an improvement for the leading actors because whereas the Cold War could not be sustained once the USSR had imploded and international communism had toppled into the dust bin of history, a war on terrorism, with all its associated benefits, can go on forever. After all, so long as the president says that he has intelligence information to the effect that "they" are still out there conspiring to kill us all, who are we to dispute that the threat exists and must be met? The smoke had scarcely cleared at Ground Zero when Vice President Dick Cheney declared on October 19, 2001, that the war on terrorism "may never end. It's the new normalcy."

Just as during the Cold War hardly any American ever laid eyes on an honest-to-God Commie, although nearly everybody believed that the Commies were lurking far and wide, so now we may all suppose that anyone, anywhere, might be a lethal terrorist in possession of a suitcase nuke or a jug of anthrax spores. Indeed, current airport-security measures are premised on precisely such a belief—otherwise, it makes no sense to strip-search Grandma at Dulles International.

Potential terrorists are "out there," no doubt, in the wonderful world of Islam, an arc that stretches from Morocco across North Africa, the Middle East, and Southwest Asia to Malaysia, and on through Indonesia to Mindanao, not to mention London, Amsterdam, and Hamburg. And that's good, because it means that U.S. leaders must bring the entire outside world into compliance with their stipulated rules of engagement for the war on terrorism. It's a fine thing to dominate the world, an even finer thing to do so righteously.

Better yet, the potential omnipresence of the terrorists justifies

U.S. leaders in their efforts to supercharge the surveillance and police state here at home, with the USA PATRIOT Act, the revival of the FBI's COINTELPRO activities, and all the rest. Adios Bill of Rights. The merest babe understands that these new powers will be turned to other political purposes that have nothing whatever to do with terrorism. Indeed, they have been already. As the *New York Times* reported on May 5, 2003, "the Justice Department has begun using its expanded counterterrorism powers to seize millions of dollars from foreign banks that do business in the United States," and "most of the seizures have involved fraud and money-laundering investigations unrelated to terrorism."

The "war on terrorism" rationale has proved congenial to the American public, who have swallowed bogus government assurances that the so-called war is making them more secure. Much of this acceptance springs, no doubt, from the shock that many Americans experienced when the terrorist attacks of September 11 proved so devastating. Ever alert, the president's national-security adviser Condoleezza Rice asked the National Security Council immediately afterward "to think seriously about 'how do you capitalize on these opportunities' to fundamentally change American doctrine and the shape of the world in the wake of September 11." The president's most powerful and influential subordinates—Cheney, Donald Rumsfeld, Paul Wolfowitz, and their coterie—then set in motion a series of actions (and a flood of disinformation) to seize the day, measures that culminated in the military invasion and conquest of Afghanistan and then of Iraq, among many other things. Public-opinion polls continue to show exceptionally high approval ratings for "the job the president is doing," so at the White House everyone is merry indeed.

Likewise, the military component of the MICC has entered into fat city. During the fiscal year 2000, before George Bush had taken office, Department of Defense outlays amounted to $281 billion. Just four years later, assuming that Congress gives the president what he has requested for fiscal year 2004, the department's budget will be at least $399 billion—an increase of 42 percent. No wonder the generals and admirals are dancing in the corridors at the Pentagon: all this loot and wartime citations and promotions to boot!

The flush times for the officer corps have spilled over handsomely onto the big arms contractors, whose share prices have been bucking the trend of the continuing stock-market meltdown nicely during the past couple years. With only a single exception, all the major weapons systems have survived funding threats, and their manufacturers can look forward to decades of well-paid repose as they supply models B, C, D, and so forth, as well as all the remunerative maintenance and repairs, operational training, software upgrades, and related goods and services for their Cold War–type weaponry in search of a suitable enemy. In the immortal words of Boeing vice president Harry Stonecipher, "the purse is now open." As the *Wall Street Journal* reported, "The antiterror campaign is making for some remarkably flush times for the military, and the need for hard choices on weapons systems has all but evaporated."

Congress savors this situation, too. In the current circumstances, the members can more easily use spending on guns to grease their own reelection skids. "In a bipartisan voice," reported the *New York Times,* "lawmakers on Capitol Hill are telling the Pentagon that they want to increase spending on conventional big-ticket weapons programs, particularly warships and planes." Moreover, many members continue to maneuver to stop or delay base closures that might save the Pentagon billions of dollars in expenses that even the generals regard as pointless.

Amid the all-around rejoicing, however, the power elite appreciate that nearly two years have elapsed since September 11, 2001, and the public's panic has begun to subside. That won't do. Accordingly, on June 9 the government released a report that there is a "high probability" of an al Qaeda attack with a weapon of mass destruction in the next two years. If no such attack should eventuate, of course, then the authorities will have to release another such terrifying report at the appropriate time. Got to keep people on their toes—"vigilant," as the Homeland Security czar likes to say.

So there you have it: the war on terrorism—the new permanent war—is a winner. The president loves it. The military brass love it. The bigwigs at Boeing and Lockheed love it. Members of Congress love it. The public loves it. We all love it.

Except, perhaps, that odd citizen who wonders whether, all things considered, having a permanent war is truly a good idea for the beleaguered U.S. economy and for the liberties of the American people.

20

How Does the War Party Get Away with It?

If you see someone shuffling along the street, eyes downcast, a pained expression on his face, you may have stumbled upon a member of the Peace Party. Once again, this party's cause has gone down to defeat, and its members are shaking their heads sadly, wondering why.

Their anguish is not assuaged by the knowledge that ultimately many will come to see that they were right to oppose this war. Eventual vindication will avail them little. The war is a fait accompli, and time's arrow flies in only one direction. The death, destruction, and misery that the war has caused cannot be erased. On the contrary, for many of the victims, that misery will only fester, despoiling the other lives it touches, just as it did in the aftermath of earlier, similarly mistaken wars. Think of all the former soldiers with parts of their bodies missing or parts of their minds gone askew. In this country, veterans' institutions brim with these enduring casualties, and big-city alleys harbor no small number of them. In Iraq, the innocent victims of this year's war are counted in the tens of thousands, and their number continues to mount.

While the architects of war, the Cheneys, Rumsfelds, and Wolfowitzs, who sleep every night between clean sheets, deem these terrible costs to be worth bearing—as well they might, because they personally bear not an ounce of them—the members of the Peace Party often seem baffled. In view of the evident futility, and worse, of nearly every war the United States has fought during the past century, how does the War Party manage to propel this nation into one catastrophe after another, each of them clearly foreseen by at least a substantial minority who failed to dissuade their fellow citizens from still another march into calamity?

An adequate answer might fill a volume, but some elements of that answer can be sketched briefly. The essential components are autocratic government, favorably disposed mass culture, public ignorance and misplaced trust, cooperative mass media, and political exploitation for personal and institutional advantage.

By "autocratic government," I refer to the reality of how foreign policy is actually made in the United States. Notwithstanding the trappings of our political system's democratic procedures, checks and balances, elections, and so forth, the making of foreign policy involves only a handful of people decisively. When the president and his coterie of top advisers decide to go to war, they just go, and nobody can stop them. The "intelligence" agencies, the diplomatic corps, and the armed forces do as they are told. Members of Congress cower and speak in mealy-mouthed phrases framed to ensure that no matter how the war turns out, they can share any credit and deny any blame. No one has effective capacity to block the president, and few officials care to do so in any event, even if they object. Rarely does anyone display the minimal decency of resigning his military commission or his appointment in the bureaucracy. In short, in our system the president has come to hold the power of war and peace exclusively in his hands, notwithstanding anything to the contrary written in the Constitution or the laws. He might as well be Caesar.

(In the late 1930s, Congress considered the Ludlow Resolution, which would have amended the Constitution to require approval in a national referendum before Congress could declare war, unless U.S. territory had been invaded. Franklin D. Roosevelt vigorously opposed such an amendment, writing to the Speaker of the House on January 6, 1938, that its adoption "would cripple any President in his conduct of our foreign relations," and the resolution was narrowly voted down [209 to 188] in the House soon afterward. Can't let the inmates run the asylum, now can we?)

Of course, eventually the president who projects the country into war may have to stand for reelection, and he or at least his party may be repudiated for the war making. Such a denouement occurred in 1920, 1952, 1968, and perhaps in 1992. Although on such occasions some observers always conclude that "the system worked," nothing could be further from the truth, because by the time the voters repudiate the leader responsible for plunging the nation into a senseless war, the damage has been done and cannot be undone. Wilson gained reelection in 1916 as the candidate who had "kept us out of war," then immediately reversed himself, and four years later his party was turned out of the presidency. Too late then, however. Lyndon Baines Johnson campaigned against sending "American boys to do the job that Asian boys should do," then immediately reversed himself, and four years later his party was turned out of the presidency. Again, much too late. Elections simply cannot control the autocracy of U.S. presidents in deciding whether to go to war, and ex post electoral discipline counts for next to nothing.

Presidents decide to go to war in the context of a favorably disposed mass culture. Painful as it is for members of the Peace Party to admit, many Americans take pleasure in "kicking ass," and they do not much care whose ass is being kicked or why. So long as Americans are dishing out death and destruction to a plausible foreign enemy, the red-white-and-blue jingos are happy. If you think I'm engaging in hyperbole, you need to get out more. Visit a barbershop, stand in line at the post office, or have a drink at your neighborhood tavern and listen to the conversations going on around you. The sheer bellicosity of many ordinary people's views is as undeniable as it is shocking. Something in their diet seems to be causing a remarkable volume of murderous, barely suppressed rage.

An eagerness to spill blood and guts extends, however, well beyond the rednecks. Highly literate, albeit sophistic, expressions of this proclivity appear nearly every day on the editorial page of the *Wall Street Journal,* a Likud Party megaphone whose motto might well be "all wars all the time." Establishment think thanks, most notably the American Enterprise Institute, trot out well-spoken intellectuals in squads to trumpet the necessity of wreaking global death and destruction.

No one should be surprised by the cultural proclivity for violence, of course, because Americans have always been a violent people in a violent land. Once the Europeans committed themselves to reside on this continent, they undertook to slaughter the Indians and steal their land, and to bullwhip African slaves into submission and live off their labor—endeavors they pursued with considerable success over the next two and a half centuries. Absent other convenient victims, they have battered and killed one another on the slightest pretext, or for the simple pleasure of doing so, with guns, knives, and bare hands. If you take them to be a "peace-loving people," you haven't been paying attention. Such violent people are easily led to war.

Public ignorance compounds the inclinations fostered by the mass culture. Study after study and poll after poll have confirmed that most Americans know next to nothing about public affairs. Of course, the intricacies of foreign policy are as alien to them as the dark side of the moon, but their ignorance runs much deeper. They can't explain the simplest elements of the political system; they don't know what the Constitution says or means; and they can't identify their political representatives or what those persons ostensibly stand for. They know scarcely anything about history, and what they think they know is usually incorrect. People so densely ignorant that they have no inkling of how their forebears were bamboozled and sacrificed on the altar of Mars the last time around are easily bamboozled and readily sacrificed the next time around.

Forming a snowcap on this mountain of ignorance is a widespread willingness to trust governing authorities, especially the president. Thus, if President Bush tells the people that Iraq poses a serious threat to the United States, many of them believe him. Presidents and their lieutenants exploit this misplaced trust to gain popular approval for bellicose foreign policies, knowing that even if every somewhat educated or skeptical person in the country opposes the policy, it nevertheless will receive substantial support in the polls.

So long as war is something that happens "out there" somewhere, most likely in a place that few Americans have ever visited and most can't even locate on a map, and not too many body bags are delivered with sons and husbands inside, then the masses tend to find sufficient bliss in their ignorance and childlike trust in their rulers. Flag waving and other symbolic displays bring them a cheap solidary identification with the great nation-state, but few have any immediate contact with events in the empire. As an issue, war remains foreign to them in the literal sense—always somebody else's problem.

Cooperative news media help the rulers to market their war making. The big media, enjoying entrenched positions in the established order, are reluctant to challenge the government's foreign aggressiveness. At the working level, reporters do not want to be cut off from privileged access to inside sources of information. At the upper level, owners and producers do not wish to seem unpatriotic, as the government might label them if pushed too hard. Of course, in any event, profit-seeking media are bound to tailor their product to the sort of readers, listeners, or viewers to whom they cater. Thus, among the bottom feeders, Fox News quite rationally aims to entertain the bloodthirsty yahoos; and in the upper reaches, the *New York Times* knows better than to offend strong supporters of the state of Israel. Although many sources of news and analysis exist nowadays, especially on the World Wide Web, and some of them stoutly oppose senseless belligerence, people must invest time and energy to seek out such alternatives, and relatively few people do so.

Finally, we must recognize that for many persons and institutions, war is a good deal. Hence, each foreign adventure provides a splendid opportunity for many to gain personal, political, or economic profit. The so-called war on terror has been a godsend for everybody who purports to be in the security business, from data-management specialists to security personnel–training firms to the manufacturers of surveillance machinery, not to mention all those new hires at the Department of Homeland Security and the Department of Justice. At Oracle, a company with roots in service to the CIA, Larry Ellison is gunning to equip the government with software that will allow the authorities to track your every move, but this nefarious company is hardly the only opportunist on the block.

The entire Bush administration was wallowing without a breeze in its sails until September 11 came along and gave its head man an excuse for "greatness." Now the vacuous George W. Bush has been elevated to the status of a virtual Winston Churchill shouting across the English Channel, "Bring 'em on," and nonentities such as Tom Ridge have become household words. Campaign genius Karl Rove is banking on the president's martial leadership to bring home the electoral bacon for Republicans in 2004. For all those associated with the Bushies and their cronies in the military-industrial complex and other pet industries and professions, these are happy days indeed.

To cover their tracks, the leaders of the War Party are relying on Machiavelli's wisdom, which tells them: "It is necessary . . . to be a great pretender and dissembler; and men are so simple, and so subject to present necessities, that he who seeks to deceive will always find someone who will allow himself to be deceived." Pretending to cut taxes, wildly increasing federal spending for nearly every species of boondoggle (thus buying off potential Democratic opponents in Congress), hiking the deficit, and shoving the burden of servicing the resultant public debt onto future generations of taxpayers, they understand well the classic expression of political irresponsibility: "apres nous le deluge." Those high waters will be somebody else's problem then, and, if the future repeats the past, few of the unfortunate souls who find themselves immersed will look back and blame the true culprits.

21

The Defense Budget Is Bigger Than You Think

When President Bush signed the defense authorization bill for fiscal year 2004 on November 24, 2003, the event received considerable attention in the news media. At $401.3 billion, the public's visible cost of funding the nation's defense seemed to be reaching astronomical heights, and the president took pains to justify that enormous cost by linking it to the horrors of 9/11 and to the "war on terror." He pledged that "we will do whatever it takes to keep our nation strong, to keep the peace, and to keep the American people secure," clearly implying that such payoffs would accrue from the expenditures and other measures that the act authorizes.

Although the public may appreciate that $401.3 billion is a great deal of money, few citizens realize that it is only part of the total bill for defense. Lodged elsewhere in the budget, other lines identify funding that serves defense purposes just as surely as—sometimes even more surely than—the money allocated to the Department of Defense (DoD). On occasion, commentators take note of some of these additional defense-related budget items, such as the nuclear-weapons activities of the Department of Energy (DoE), but many such items, including some extremely large ones, remain generally unrecognized.

Since the creation of the Department of Homeland Security (DHS), many observers probably would agree that its budget ought to be included in any complete accounting of defense costs. After all, the homeland is what most of us want the government to defend in the first place.

Many other agencies, such as the Department of Justice and the Department of Transportation, also spend money in pursuit of homeland security. According to the government's budget documents (*Budget of the United States Government, Fiscal Year 2004,* table S-5), in fiscal year 2002 all such agencies together added approximately 50 percent to the amount spent on homeland security by the agencies later incorporated into the DHS.

Much of the budget for the Department of State and for international assistance programs ought to be classified as defense related, too. In this case, the money serves to buy off potential enemies and to reward friendly governments who assist U.S. efforts to abate perceived threats. A great deal of U.S. foreign aid, currently more than $4 billion annually, takes the form of "foreign military financing," and even funds placed under the rubric of economic development may serve defense-related purposes indirectly. Money is fungible, and the receipt of foreign assistance for economic-development projects allows allied governments to divert other funds to police, intelligence, and military purposes.

Two big budget items represent the current cost of defense goods and services obtained in the past. The Department of Veterans Affairs (DVA), which is authorized to spend more than $62 billion in the current fiscal year, falls into this category. Likewise, much of the government's interest expense represents the current cost of defense outlays financed in the past by borrowing.

To estimate the size of the entire de facto defense budget, I have gathered data for fiscal year 2002, the most recent fiscal year for which data on actual outlays were available at the time of this writing. In that fiscal year, the DoD itself spent $344.4 billion. Defense-related parts of the DoE budget added $18.5 billion. Agencies later to be incorporated into the DHS spent $17.5 billion, and other agencies (not including the DoD) added $8.5 billion for homeland security. The Department of State and international assistance programs spent $17.6 billion for activities arguably related to defense purposes either directly or indirectly. The DVA had outlays of $50.9 billion. When all these other parts of the budget are added to the budget for the DoD itself, they increase the total by nearly a third, to $457.4 billion.

To find out how much of the government's net interest payments on the national debt ought to be attributed to past debt-funded defense spending requires a considerable amount of calculation. I have added up all past deficits (minus surpluses) since 1916 (when the debt was nearly zero), prorated according to each year's ratio of national-security spending—military, veterans, and international affairs—to total federal spending, expressing everything in dollars of constant purchasing power. This sum is equal to 81.1 percent of the value of the national debt held by the public in 2002. Therefore, I attribute that same percentage of the government's net interest outlays in that year to past debt-financed defense spending. The total amount so attributed comes to $138.7 billion.

Adding this interest component to the previous all-agency total, the grand total comes to $596.1 billion, which is more than 73 percent greater than DoD outlays alone.

If the additional elements of defense spending continue to maintain approximately the same ratio to the DoD amount—and we have every reason to suppose that they will—then in fiscal year 2004, through which we are passing currently, the grand total spent for defense will be approximately $695 billion. To this amount will have to be added the $58.8 billion allocated to fiscal year 2004 from the $87.5 billion supplemental spending authorized on November 6, 2003, for support of U.S. military actions in Afghanistan and Iraq and for so-called reconstruction of those despoiled and occupied countries. Thus, the super–grand total in fiscal year 2004 will reach the astonishing amount of nearly $754 billion—or 88 percent more than the much-publicized $401.3 billion—plus, of course, any additional supplemental spending that may be approved before the end of the fiscal year.

Although I have arrived at my conclusions honestly and carefully, I may have left out items that should have been included—the federal budget is a gargantuan, complex, and confusing document. If I have done so, however, the left-out items are not likely to be relatively large ones. Therefore, I propose that in any consideration of future defense budgetary costs, a well-founded rule of thumb is to take the Pentagon's (always well-publicized) basic budget total and double it. You may overstate the truth, but, if so, you'll not do so by much.

Defense Outlays in Fiscal Year 2002	(billions of dollars)
Department of Defense	344.4
Department of Energy	18.5
Department of State	17.6
Department of Veterans Affairs	50.9
Agencies incorporated into Department of Homeland Security	17.5
Department of Justice (homeland security)	2.1
Department of Transportation (homeland security)	1.4
Department of the Treasury (homeland security)	0.1
National Aeronautics and Space Administration (homeland security)	0.2
Other agencies (homeland security)	4.7
Interest attributable to past debt-financed defense outlays	138.7
Total	596.1

Sources: Author's classifications and calculations; basic data from U.S. Office of Management and Budget, *Budget of the United States Government, Fiscal Year 2004,* and U.S. Bureau of the Census, *Historical Statistics of the United States, Colonial Times to 1970.*

PART V

Bush and the Bushies

22

The President Is Reading a Book, I'm Afraid

President George W. Bush has been reading a book. At least, he claims to have been reading one. I know what you're thinking, but the First Shrub swears that he has been reading more than just the funny papers lately. We'd all be better off, however, if he had stuck to the comics.

In an interview with an Associated Press reporter, Bush said that on his vacation he had been reading a recently published book by Eliot A. Cohen, *The Supreme Command: Soldiers, Statesmen, and Leadership in Wartime.* Cohen is a well-known neocon war hawk and all-around armchair warrior who professes "strategic studies" at the Johns Hopkins University School of Advanced International Studies and, in his spare time, ponders megadeaths (his own not included) with other lusty members of the Defense Policy Board. The quintessential civilian go-getter, he never met a war he didn't want to send somebody else to fight and die in.

The Supreme Command consists of case studies of how four "statesmen"—Abraham Lincoln, Georges Clemenceau, Winston Churchill, and David Ben-Gurion—successfully managed to make their generals act more vigorously than those officers really wanted to act. By spurring their too-timid generals, these four micromanaging commanders in chief supposedly got superior results from their war-making efforts. The common soldiers who were fed into the consuming maw of war under these worthies might have given us a different opinion, but dead men don't make good critics.

So what are we to make of Bush's reading of this book, assuming that he really has been reading it? The short answer is that this is not good news for the world. Such reading seems calculated to bend the president's mind, never a mighty organ in any event, toward thinking of himself in Lincolnian or Churchillian terms. Indeed, those of us who have had the stomach to observe his public strutting and puffing since September 11 might have suspected that his juvenile sensibilities would be drawn all too readily toward such a grandiose self-conception. After all, does he but speak, and mighty armadas are launched on a global war against evil?

As he clears brush at his Texas digs and takes his jogs with the Secret Service boys, Bush may fancy that he is cut from the same cloth as his Republican predecessor Theodore Roosevelt—he of the strenuous life and the more than a bit balmy conception of man's relation to his fellow man, most of whom he would gladly crush like bugs under his manly jackboots. Why worry, the current president might be thinking, about the views of a wimp such as Colin Powell? What does he know about war, in comparison with, say, Richard Perle and Paul Wolfowitz, whose heroic military service has long been the stuff of legend?

Unfortunately for the world, the president's bedtime perusal of Cohen's *Supreme Command* may set his childish imagination aflame with visions of Great Statesmanship. "Damn," he may think, expelling a masculine expletive, "I too can be a Lincoln or a Churchill." Devoutly may we all hope that the opportunity evades him, for both of those storied "statesmen" were monsters whose hands were stained beyond cleansing with innocent blood. Yet a man would need an adult sensibility to understand such realities, and Bush II, it seems clear, has a mind that never matured, if indeed it had the potential for such maturation in the first place. Manifestly, he is but a boy playing with immense, lethal toys. Yet when he says jump, legions of heavily armed men ask: How high?

When word got out that Bush was reading a book, reporters sought out gurus to cogitate on this strange development and to cough up appraisals, and those gurus, being deep thinkers, could not resist suggesting other books that the president might profitably read, should he ever decide again to read a book. One talking head recommended Sun Tzu's *Art of War.* Another touted *October Fury,* Peter Huchthausen's book on the Cuban missile crisis. Still another sage pointed to Churchill's volumes on World War II, as if the Shrub were capable of such heavy lifting.

Very well, I can play this game. I recommend that the president read "The Constitution of the United States." It's short; he can handle it. And, after all, it's what he swore to "preserve, protect, and defend" when he took office, so he might have some interest in reading it. If he's really pressed for time, he can skip everything except Article II, Section 2, which in just three short paragraphs describes the constitutional duties of the president of the United States. Sure enough, as the president's flunkies never cease telling the press, the president's first constitutional power is to "be Commander in Chief of the Army and Navy." But that's all, along those lines: just to be commander in chief. There's not even so much as a hint that the president has constitutional authority to commit the country to war—that power is obviously lodged in Article I, where the powers of Congress are enumerated. Certainly, the Constitution does not authorize the executive to engage the nation's armed forces in a "preemptive war" against Iraq, a small, impoverished country halfway around the world that does not now pose a serious threat to the security of the American people who have the wit to steer clear of it and its immediate environs.

If the president should want to read further, perhaps to find out how the powers of the presidency have been so vastly and unjustifiably enlarged over time, until presidents now consider themselves warranted in acting as absolute tyrants over their own people and those of other countries as well, he might well read two books edited by John V. Denson, *The Costs of War* (1997) and *Reassessing the Presidency* (2001).

Clemenceau famously declared that war is too important to be left to the generals. It's a no-brainer to see that war is too important to be left to the likes of Bush, Cohen, Perle, Wolfowitz, and company.

23

George Bush's Faith-Based Foreign Policy

In public statements, President George W. Bush has often avowed his personal religious faith, and from the very beginning of his administration he has sought to draw churches and other religious organizations into the orbit of the government's provision of goods and services—thus, the so-called faith-based initiatives. Bush insists that such religious providers have an excellent record in helping drug addicts and others who have gone astray to get their lives back on track. Although the president has yet to announce formally that his foreign policy also relies heavily on faith, this reality has become increasingly clear as his term in office has unfolded.

When the administration released its "National Security Strategy of the United States of America" to Congress last summer, the grandiosity of the intentions expressed in the document stunned many observers—as Mises Institute historian Joseph Stromberg noted, "it must be read to be believed." The strategy amounts to an enormously presumptuous agenda for domination of the entire world, not only overweening in the vast scope of the specific ambitions enumerated, but also brazen in the implicit assumption that the president of the United States and his lieutenants are morally entitled to run the planet. It takes a lot of faith in one's own rectitude to declare, among other things, that "our best defense is a good offense" (I am not making this up; it's in the document). Small wonder that George Bush closes his introduction to the document by resorting to religious metaphor, referring to his foreign policy as "this great mission."

Well might we recall, however, that the crusaders of old went forth on their faith-inspired missions heavily armed and itching for a fight, and in those respects the Bush administration bears a startling resemblance to them. "As a matter of common sense and self-defense, America will act against . . . emerging threats before they are fully formed," the president declares. In disturbingly Orwellian rhetoric, he affirms that "the only path to peace and security is the path of action"—the path, that is, of launching unprovoked military attacks on other countries. This ongoing preemption, supported by the administration's faith that it can identify the threats correctly even before they blossom, will be, the president warns, "a global enterprise of uncertain duration." We may presume that once Eurasia has been preemptively polished off, the United States will set its military sights on Eastasia.

The administration's faith in preemptive warfare currently expresses itself in the plan for military conquest of Iraq, a country that has not threatened the United States and does not possess the means to do so effectively in any event (in part because the United States has been waging low-level warfare and enforcing an economic embargo against it for some twelve years). The Cheney-Rumsfeld-Wolfowitz-Perle coterie evidently has faith that the United States can conquer Iraq quickly and then turn it into a showcase of stable, flourishing democracy. The sheer preposterousness of this expectation suggests that it is fueled more by quasi-religious zealotry than by logic and evidence. Whatever else Iraq may be, it certainly is not a democratic success story waiting to be told by American crusaders. Indeed, given the violent ethnic, religious, and political conflicts that ravage this unfortunate country, it may not be viable under any form of government except dictatorship—nothing in its history suggests otherwise.

Nonetheless, President Bush, after having insisted not so long ago that he opposed getting our country bogged down in utopian "nation building," now has unleashed the neoconservative fanatics to transform the Middle East into a fantastical form they find pleasing, molding Iraq itself into something remarkably like the placid social democracies of North America and western Europe. If you suspect that the Iraqis lack the necessary parts to compose this visionary contraption, well, you just need to have faith. As St. Paul wrote to the Hebrews (11:1), "faith is the substance of things hoped for, the evidence of things not seen"—a characterization that fits perfectly the administration's vertiginous conception of the postconquest reconstruction of Iraq.

Finally, the Bush administration has faith that it can continue to drag the American people down the path of perpetual war for perpetual peace and endless nation building. Maybe it can: for the most part, the people certainly have rolled over and played patsy so far, especially if we judge by the actions of their pusillanimous representatives in Congress, who hastened to pass a resolution unconstitutionally delegating to the president their power to declare war against Iraq.

In the past, however, the American public has risen up from time to time to insist, with regard to some disastrous foreign adventure, that enough is enough. They eventually did so during the Korean War, and they did so again during the Vietnam War. Unfortunately, in both instances the public came to its senses only after enormous loss of life and other human and material devastation had been sustained. More recently, with respect to the U.S. military mission to Somalia, the public quickly decided against spilling additional blood in a seemingly hopeless nation-building effort.

I would like to believe that sooner or later the American people will resist, and resist strongly, the Bush administration's crusade for global domination in general and its present plan to conquer and reconstruct Iraq in particular. As matters now stand, though, I just don't have much faith in the majority of my fellow citizens.

24

On Crackpot Realism

An Homage to C. Wright Mills

When I first began to read serious books on politics and government, back in the 1960s, I fell into much admiration for the writings of the New Left sociologist C. Wright Mills. He is probably best remembered for his variant of elite theory, as laid out in his book *The Power Elite* (Oxford University Press, 1956), but he influenced me at least as much by what he wrote in *The Sociological Imagination* (Oxford University Press, 1959). Between those two volumes, however, he wrote a little book called *The Causes of World War Three* (Simon and Schuster, 1958). In that passionate and ideologically inspired tract, Mills explicated a concept that I have called to mind frequently over the years—never more, however, than in the past year and a half: the concept of "crackpot realism."

For Mills, this signified a frame of mind characteristic of what another elite theorist, Thomas R. Dye, has called "the serious people" of the governing circles. Such people are to be distinguished from the glad-handing, back-slapping buffoons who seek and gain election to public office. The electoral office seekers are specialists: they know how to get votes, but as a rule they know nothing about how to "run a railroad," whether that railroad be a business, a government agency, or any other sort of large operating organization. So, after the election, the elected officeholders always turn to the serious people to run the show—the Dick Cheneys and the Donald Rumsfelds, to pick not so randomly from the current corps.

The serious people always pretend to be the grownups, as opposed to the starry-eyed rest of us, who couldn't run Halliburton or G. D. Searle & Co. if our lives depended on it. These are the sorts of executives who are tempted to and sometimes actually do roll their eyes at the silly questions journalists ask them at press conferences. Visibly pained by the necessity of spelling out the facts of life, they explain that childish things, such as keeping the country at peace, simply won't get the job done. Sometimes the public must recognize that as a no-nonsense response to the harsh situation we face, the serious people have to drop some bombs here and there in order to reestablish a proper arrangement of the world's currently disordered affairs. The serious people are frequently to be found "stabilizing" something or other.

Trouble is, Mills explained, these serious people are fools. They seem to know what's going on and how to right what's wrong with the world only if one accepts their own view of how the world works. So "practical" are these serious people, however, that they understand nothing beyond their noses and outside the circle of their own constricted understanding and experience. Strange to say, the power elite does not get out much—remember the first President Bush's amazement when he, a former CIA director, visited a supermarket and encountered for the first time the mind-boggling technology of a bar-code reader at the checkout counter. Especially when these movers and shakers deal with matters of war and peace, they continue to make the same sorts of disastrous decisions over and over, constantly squandering opportunities to maintain the peace, almost invariably painting themselves into corners of their own making, and all too often deciding that the only option that makes sense in their predicament is to bomb their way out.

As my education continued, I outgrew many of the lessons I had learned from Mills, whose own understanding of social science was flawed in various ways. Still, he had some powerful insights, especially about political sociology, and even today I do not hesitate to recommend that young scholars read his major works. Among the more timeless of his insights, I believe, is his understanding of crackpot realism. I extract a few lines here to illustrate his thinking about this matter (taken from pp. 86–88 of *The Causes of World War Three*).

As you read these thoughts, consider whether they might be as applicable today as they were forty-five years ago.

> In crackpot realism, a high-flying moral rhetoric is joined with an opportunist crawling among a great scatter of unfocused fears and demands. In fact, the main content of "politics" is now a struggle among men equally expert in practical next steps—which, in summary, make up the thrust toward war—and in great, round, hortatory principles. (p. 86)

> The expectation of war solves many problems of the crackpot realists; it also confronts them with many new problems. Yet these, the problems of war, often seem easier to handle. They are out in the open: to produce more, to plan how to kill more of the enemy, to move materials thousands of miles. . . . So instead of the unknown fear, the anxiety without end, some men of the higher circles prefer the simplification of known catastrophe. (p. 87)

> They know of no solutions to the paradoxes of the Middle East and Europe, the Far East and Africa except the landing of Marines. Being baffled, and also being very tired of being baffled, they have come to believe that there is no way out—except war—which would remove all the bewildering paradoxes of their tedious and now misguided attempts to construct peace. In place of these paradoxes they prefer the bright, clear problems of war—as they used to be. For they still believe that "winning" means something, although they never tell us what. (p. 88)

> Some men want war for sordid, others for idealistic, reasons; some for personal gain, others for impersonal principle. But most of those who consciously want war and accept it, and so help to create its "inevitability," want it in order to shift the locus of their problems. (p. 88)

Besides Mills's own writings, readers interested in his ideas may wish to read the well-done biography by Irving Louis Horowitz, *C. Wright Mills: An American Utopian* (Free Press, 1983).

25

Camelot and the Bushies
Some Disturbing Parallels

In the mythology that many Americans still cherish, the Kennedy administration was manned by suave, smart, and sophisticated people, from the cleverly articulate and frightfully handsome young president himself to the razor-sharp advisers such as Harvard's McGeorge Bundy and MIT's Walt Whitman Rostow to the steel-trap-rational cabinet officers such as Dean Rusk and Robert McNamara, in whose hands electronic computers and "systems analysis" promised to provide answers to even the most complicated socioeconomic and military questions. Not only were these men "the best and the brightest," but many of them were young and dashing, too, relishing the company of Green Berets and others engaged in derring-do.

No one, to my knowledge, has perceived any substantial similarity between the lords of Camelot and the not-so-suave characters now ruling Washington. With his inability to utter even the simplest English sentence comfortably and correctly, George W. Bush will never be mistaken for JFK redux. Nor do Dick Cheney and Donald Rumsfeld call to mind qualities of analytical genius—political shrewdness and Machiavellian cunning, perhaps, but hardly a trace of the cold, calculating, systems-analysis sort of intelligence for which McNamara's "whiz kids" were renowned. Whereas Jack Kennedy rested his faith on two millennia of Catholic doctrine and ceremony, George Bush is a relative religious primitive, a Methodist and, he claims, "born again."

Yet, notwithstanding all the apparent dissimilarities between these two ruling gangs, they display some disturbing similarities as well. These parallels hit me hard recently as I was reading Derek

Leebaert's new history of the Cold War, *The Fifty-Year Wound* (Little, Brown, 2002). Leebaert brings into sharp relief some hallmarks of the Kennedy administration that have tended to be suppressed or given a falsely positive gloss by the many who have adulated the martyred president and his brief regime.

The Kennedy people reeked of recklessness, not just in their personal lives, where it could be kept out of sight or excused, but in their policymaking. "The youthful and vigorous men who came to power in January [1961]," writes Leebaert, "saw few limits and acted accordingly" (p. 256). Thus, they plowed ahead with the foolhardy, ill-prepared, and ultimately disastrous Bay of Pigs invasion. They senselessly pushed the world to the brink of nuclear catastrophe in their management of the Cuban missile crisis. President Kennedy's—and his brother Robert's—obsession with killing Fidel Castro, an objective that went unrealized despite countless comic-opera CIA plots to do the dirty work, so twisted their judgment that it gave rise to more than a few policy pretzels.

Reckless in his dealings with the Cubans and the Soviets, Kennedy was no more level-headed in dealing with the situation in Southeast Asia. Above all, however, the mock-virile president resolved that he must demonstrate toughness. He kept increasing the number of U.S. troops in South Vietnam—from 692 when he took office to nearly 17,000 at the time of his death. By that time, too, more ominously, some one million U.S. troops had been stationed at more than two hundred foreign bases scattered around the globe.

The quintessential Cold Warrior and "a frightening risk taker" (p. 260), Kennedy suffered "no shortage of adrenaline, violence, or noble intentions" (p. 258). Not surprisingly, therefore, he failed to keep the military on a short civilian leash at a time when nutcase generals cut from the molds of Curtis LeMay, Thomas Power, and Lyman Lemnitzer were running the show. "The Pentagon was taking dangerous operational shortcuts," Leebaert writes, "such as putting thousands of [nuclear] weapons on hair-trigger alert, and men outside the legal chain of presidential succession would have been able to decide to launch them" (p. 317). It is worthwhile to recall that the classic Cold War film *Dr. Strangelove* depicts conditions as they existed during the Kennedy administration (though in the film President Merkin Muffley, oddly enough, bears a close resemblance to Adlai Stevenson).

The Kennedy administration's leaders displayed, in Leebaert's phrase, "an astonishing militancy" (p. 256). Yet, despite their high-toned educations and their polished social graces, they generally had only the foggiest idea what they were doing—they epitomized what the sociologist C. Wright Mills called "crackpot realism." Hence, "misjudgment became inescapable as emergency moved further into a dramatizable, institutionally underwritten way of life" (p. 257). From the bloody fiasco of the Bay of Pigs at the outset to the near-doomsday disaster of the missile crisis to the heedless plunge into the quicksand of Vietnam, these best and brightest "people whom the opportunities offered by the modern state tempt[ed] into an eternal trifling with danger and extremity" (p. 261) proceeded from one blunder to the next during "those strutting years" (p. 262).

The Kennedy people concealed their colossal foreign-policy mismanagement behind a parapet of prevarication—lies about responsibility for the Bay of Pigs, lies about what had happened in connection with the occurrence and the resolution of the missile crisis, lies about what the U.S. "advisers" and the CIA operatives were actually doing in Southeast Asia. Little did the American people imagine just how massively and how routinely their government was misleading them about its malodorous doings abroad. Thus, ordinary Americans failed to suspect that "good people" such as themselves might now be involved in political murders and related transgressions around the world on a daily basis—all part of the Kennedy administration's emphasis on "counterinsurgency," a global program in which "the endless demand for tactical responses provided government with years of temptations to deceive, or worse" (p. 301). Not content with merely responding to the communists and their real or imagined surrogates, however, President Kennedy urged his lieutenants to consider taking the first shot. Thus, he "encouraged the CIA and other government arms to explore preventive action, including plans to 'take out' China's nuclear program" (p. 311).

Against this template, the current Bush administration has come to provide a distressingly close fit. Increasingly, this government has displayed a militancy, an aggressiveness, a global ambition to fight any and all perceived enemies (except, perhaps, those that can fight back, such as North Korea), and a reliance on military force, including preventive attacks, that must have Jack Kennedy smiling somewhere in the netherworld. Even the ridiculous physical strutting that has become the characteristic presidential gait since the September 11 attacks calls to mind "those strutting years" that Leebaert associates with Kennedy's time in power.

To read the Bush administration's "National Security Strategy" is to appreciate just how much the current government reexpresses the presumptuousness and the hubris of the Kennedy administration. Now, however, we find the earlier interest in preventive attacks raised to a pillar of policy, explicitly encapsulated in the motto "the best defense is a good offense." Hence, "as a matter of common sense and self-defense," the president declares in his introduction to the document, "America will act against . . . emerging threats before they are fully formed." Just as Kennedy's whiz kids had supreme confidence in their ability to apply cost-benefit analysis to every defense-policy problem, so the Bush men have supreme confidence in their capacity to identify mortal threats even before they have blossomed.

Just as Jack Kennedy had "no shortage of adrenaline, violence, or noble intentions," so George W. Bush proclaims that "the only path to peace and security is the path of action." Just as Kennedy declared that under his heroic leadership we Americans would "pay any price, bear any burden, meet any hardship, support any friend, oppose any foe," so Bush foresees "a global enterprise of uncertain duration" and proposes to lead us courageously and full of Christian faith on "this great mission." His subordinates have been telling every talk-show host who would entertain them, however, that the upshot of their global crusade will be not a field of thorns, but a magnificent flowering of democracies as far as the eye can see, even in backward and strife-torn regions where no successful democracy has ever existed and where the political culture is wholly antithetical to such a system of government. The proffered basis for this course of action makes the Kennedy people's ignorance of Southeast Asia look almost like full information. Once again, crackpot realism sits firmly in the saddle.

If the Kennedy administration proceeded recklessly, the Bush administration seems intent on equaling or exceeding that classic recklessness. Thus, Bush and company have chosen to disregard and insult important long-time allies and to proceed unilaterally in a world the administration defines as consisting exclusively of those who are with us and those who are against us. (So much for the principle of neutrality, for which the United States went to war in 1917.) Thumbing its nose at the necessity of a UN sanction for its war against Iraq, the Bush government has the audacity to justify its aggression by pointing to Saddam Hussein's failure to comply with UN resolutions.

Finally, we come to the two administrations' matching mendacity. If Kennedy and company could stand up and lie with a straight face about nearly every action they were taking or had taken overseas, the Bush people likewise feel no evident shame in torturing the truth. Even the government's intelligence officers have complained that the political operatives keep making them rework their analyses until their conclusions accord with the ideological predispositions of Cheney, Rumsfeld, Wolfowitz, and the rest of the neoconservative fanatics leading the charge for imperialism. When veteran foreign-service officer John Brady Kiesling resigned recently, he wrote to Secretary of State Colin Powell that "we have not seen such systematic distortion of intelligence, such systematic manipulation of American opinion, since the war in Vietnam." But Secretary Powell himself had already capitulated to the pressure and shamelessly spouted lies in his attempts to win support for U.S. aggression at the

UN. Blithely ignoring the lack of evidence, Bush himself has continued to assert that Saddam Hussein's government has a "link" with al Qaeda, that it is developing nuclear weapons, that it poses a grave threat to the United States. Lies pile upon lies, and questions are answered only with impatient bluster or a menacing smirk.

In sum, upon inspection, we can see many disturbing parallels between the energetic, world-smacking Kennedy administration and the present hyperaggressive Bush administration. May heaven help us to survive these all-too-vigorous men of action.

26

Is Bush Unhinged?

Before you conclude that I myself must be unhinged even to raise such a question, ask yourself this: If a man talks as if he has lost contact with reality, then might he actually have done so? Granted that this possibility deserves evaluation, then consider President George W. Bush's rhetoric in his March 19 speech to diplomats and others at the White House.

The president begins by stating his interpretation of the recent bombings in Madrid, reiterating one of his recurrent themes of the past two and a half years: "[T]he civilized world is at war" in a "new kind of war." The concept of war, of course, ranks high among evocative metaphors. Not by accident have politicians declared wars on poverty, drugs, cancer, illiteracy, and an assortment of other alleged enemies. A society at war, as William James observed in 1906 in his call for the "moral equivalent of war," finds a reason for unaccustomed solidarity and—here's where the politicians come in—for unaccustomed submission to central government authority. James himself, after all, was arguing that "the martial type of character can be bred without war." Political leaders are always seeking to establish such character, with themselves in command of the battalions of "disciplined" subjects. Insofar as the so-called war on terrorism merely represents the latest attempt to bend the war metaphor to an obvious political purpose, we might well dismiss the president's rhetorical flourish as nothing but the same old same old.

Bush, however, will allow no such dismissal. "The war on terror," he insists, "is not a figure of speech." Well, I beg your pardon, Mr. President, but that is precisely what it is. How can one go to war against "terror," which is a state of mind? Even if the president were to take more care with his language and to speak instead of a "war on terrorism," the phrase still could not be anything more than a metaphor because terrorism is a form of action available to virtually any determined adult anywhere anytime. War on terrorism, too, can be only a figure of speech.

War, if it is anything, is the marshalling of armed forces against somebody, not against a state of mind or a form of action. Wars are fought between groups of persons. We might argue about whether the United States can wage war only against another nation-state, as opposed to an indefinitely large number of individuals committed to fanatical Islamism who in various workaday guises are living in scores of different countries. The expression "war on certain criminals and conspirators of criminal acts" would fit the present case better and would entail far more sensible thinking about the proper way to deal with such persons. The idea of war, obviously, calls to mind too readily the serviceability of the armed forces. Hence, the application of such forces to the conquest of Iraq in the name of "bringing the terrorists to justice," although that conquest was actually nothing but a hugely destructive, immensely expensive diversion from genuine efforts to allay the threat posed by the Islamist maniacs who compose al Qaeda and similar groups. "These killers will be tracked down and found, they will face their day of justice," the president declares, speaking as always as if only a fixed number of such killers exist, rather than a vast reservoir of actual and potential recruits that is only augmented and revitalized by actions such as the U.S. invasion of Iraq. It would be a boon to humanity if the president could be brought to understand the distinction between waging war and establishing justice.

Whatever our understanding of the president's "war on terror" might be, however, he definitely parts company with reality when he states, "There is no neutral ground—no neutral ground—in the fight between civilization and terror, because there is no neutral ground between good and evil, freedom and slavery, and life and death." Of course, this Manichean pronouncement echoes the administration's previous declaration that everybody on earth is either with us or against us—and if they know what's good for them, they'll fall into line with our wishes. Aside from the undeniable fact that some nations simply prefer, as did the Spanish people (as opposed to the Aznar government), to avoid the blowback of U.S. interventions around the world, the president's insistence on equating U.S. policy with good, freedom, and life and all alternative policies with evil, slavery, and death represents the sort of childish bifurcation one expects to find expressed by a member of a youth gang, not by the leader of the world's most powerful government. To raise but a single example, though a highly relevant one in this context, can any dispassionate person argue that the U.S. position on the Israeli-Palestinian conflict is entirely good, whereas every alternative position is entirely evil?

Observers endowed with humane moral sensibilities recognize that there is plenty of evil to go around in Israel and elsewhere. In Iraq, for example, the U.S. government bears clear responsibility for killing and injuring thousands of noncombatants in the past year—not to mention the horrendous mortality and suffering it brought about previously by enforcement of the economic sanctions used to cripple that country for more than a decade. Some people maintain that the price was worth paying, that ultimately the good obtained will more than compensate for the harm caused in the process, but even if one accepts that assessment for the sake of argument, it remains true nevertheless that much harm was caused, that the burden of responsibility for evils perpetrated must be borne by the U.S. side as well as by the demonized enemy (Saddam Hussein having been made out after 1990 as "another Hitler"). International conflicts in the real world do not often divide neatly into nothing-but-good versus nothing-but-evil. For the president of the United States to employ such a juvenile characterization raises the possibility that his mind is so immature that he ought to be removed from office before he propels the world into even worse disasters.

Seemingly aware of previous criticism, the president declares that "the terrorists are offended not merely by our policies—they are offended by our existence as free nations." I myself have seen no evidence to confirm such a statement; certainly the president has adduced none. I have seen, however, the translated testimony of one Osama bin Laden, who in a famous October 2001 videotape objects to U.S. support for Israel in the Israeli-Palestinian conflict, to the presence of U.S. forces in Saudi Arabia, and to U.S. economic sanctions and other hostile actions against Iraq—that is, to various U.S. policies. "Millions of innocent children are being killed in Iraq and in Palestine and we don't hear a word from the infidels. We don't hear a raised voice," says bin Laden. In my ears, this statement sounds like an objection to U.S. policies. I have seen no evidence that bin Laden or any other known Islamic terrorist takes offence at our very existence, provided that we mind our own business in our own homeland.

In the president's mind, however, every deviation from adherence to his promulgated national-security policy of U.S. world domination and preventive warfare represents a dangerous form of appeasement: "Any sign of weakness or retreat simply validates terrorist violence, and invites more violence for all nations. The only certain way to protect our people is by early, united, and decisive action"—that is, by global military intervention by the United States, with all other nations serving as its lackeys. In the neoconservative vision to which the president has been converted, time stands still: it is always 1938, and if we fail to bring all our military might to bear preventively against the Hitler du jour, we shall certainly be plunged into global catastrophe.

Waxing positive, the president credits recent U.S. and allied military actions with bringing about "a free Afghanistan" and the "long-awaited liberation" of the Iraqi people. He maintains that

> the fall of the Iraqi dictator has removed a source of violence, aggression, and instability in the Middle East. . . . [Y]ears of illicit weapons development by the dictator have come to the end. . . . [T]he Iraqi people are now receiving

aid, instead of suffering under the sanctions. . . . [M]en and women across the Middle East, looking to Iraq, are getting a glimpse of what life in a free country can be like. . . . Who would begrudge the Iraqi people their long-awaited liberation?

This effusion evinces a tenuous grip on reality. Nobody begrudges the Iraqi people their freedom, but many of us have serious doubts about just how much freedom those long-suffering people really have. Their country is occupied by a lethal foreign army whose soldiers roam freely, breaking into homes and mosques at will, maintaining checkpoints that often become the venues of unjustified killings, carrying out police activities by employing such means as aerial bombardment and bursts of heavy machine-gun fire. If this unfortunate scene is the "glimpse of what life in a free country can be like" that others throughout the Middle East are getting, then woe unto anyone who yearns to stimulate those Middle Easterners to seek freedom. "With Afghanistan and Iraq showing the way, we are confident that freedom will lift the sights and hopes of millions in the greater Middle East," the president states. If he really harbors such confidence, one can only note how ill-founded it is.

The president seems to have no idea of what a free society consists of. Violent military occupation and the complete absence of the rule of law totally invalidate any claim that either Iraq or Afghanistan is now a free society. At present, Iraq is awash with violence perpetrated by resistance fighters and occupation forces and with criminality of all sorts unleashed by the disruptions associated with the war and by the U.S. dissolution of the old police apparatus. "We will not fail the Iraqi people, who have placed their trust in us," Bush declares. But they never placed their trust in us in the first place; they simply suffered our invasion and occupation of their country. In any event, we have already gravely disappointed the hopes that many Iraqis held for life after the overthrow of Saddam Hussein's regime. The country is rife with resentment and hostility, and the people are eager for U.S. forces to get out. Although the president maintains that "[w]e've set out to break the cycle of bitterness and radicalism that has brought stagnation to a vital region," one cannot help concluding from the facts on the ground that the upshot of the U.S. invasion and occupation has been just the opposite, that U.S. actions in Iraq have only poured fuel on the fires of terrorism there as well as in the wider world.

It is disconcerting for me to listen to the president's speeches. I get the unsettling feeling that the man inhabits another world in which things are the exact opposite of how they seem to me. Of course, I may be the one whose perspective is askew. Unlike Bush, I cannot claim that the Almighty has licensed my position. Yet I fear that time will tell in favor of my view of the matter—a view shared, of course, by most people on the planet, indeed, by nearly everybody who has not been bribed, intimidated, or blinded by partisan loyalty to the Bush administration. For now, this difference of views might seem to be nothing more than that—just one man's opinion jousting with another's—but reality has a way of passing definite judgment, and I will not be surprised if Bush's pronouncements ultimately come to be seen as having no more substance than a bad dream.

PART VI

The Road to War

27

Iraq and the United States

Who's Menacing Whom?

The recent Senate Foreign Relations Committee hearings highlight a development that ought to have inspired a great public debate, but hasn't. From the very beginning, the Bush administration has been intent on waging war against Iraq, and by now nearly the whole country seems resigned to a U.S. attack. Within the government, discussion concerns matters of timing, strategy, mobilization of military resources, provision of bases, and so forth. Hardly any prominent person has questioned the attack's underlying rationale.

Yet the justification for this war remains extremely problematic. "If we do this," said Anthony Cordesman, military guru and Iraq specialist, "it will in many ways be our first pre-emptive war. We will not have a clear smoking gun." Once upon a time, such an attack would have been labeled naked aggression; nowadays, it's swallowed with ease as the Bush Doctrine. Is everybody really in favor of a unilateral, unprovoked U.S. assault on a small, faraway country that has never attacked us and does not now pose a serious threat to us?

Ever since the buildup prior to the Gulf War, the U.S. government has undertaken to demonize Saddam Hussein. No herculean effort has been required along these lines, because by all accounts Saddam is, in fact, a murderous thug who rules Iraq with an iron fist. It stretches the limits of credulity, however, to accept characterizations of him as another Hitler. A bit of searching might turn up even more despicable leaders in other countries—Kim Jong Il, for example, whose principal occupation seems to be starving to death the North Korean people.

The presence of a murderous thug in control of a small country is hardly front-page news. Such rulers are a dime a dozen. Yet the United States does not stand on the verge of attacking all of them. What's so special about Saddam?

It is claimed, of course, that his government actively seeks to develop weapons of mass destruction—chemical, biological, and nuclear. Again, however, the same claim might be made about many countries. Moreover, many of those countries have already succeeded in developing such weapons. Yet the United States does not propose to launch attacks on India, Pakistan, China, or Russia, not to speak of France or the United Kingdom.

The story line seems to be that Saddam Hussein not only seeks to obtain weapons of mass destruction, but, once he has them, he will immediately use them against the United States. This nearly always unspoken assumption, when brought into the open, has less than overwhelming persuasive power. Why would Saddam take the assumed action? What would he gain by it?

Well, most likely, he would gain less than nothing. As former UN weapons inspector Richard Butler told the Senate Foreign Relations Committee, Saddam understands that making first use of weapons of mass destruction against the United States or its allies would guarantee his own destruction. Whatever else one may think about Saddam, no one can deny that he has been a wily leader, keenly concerned about his personal survival. He hardly qualifies as a potential suicide bomber.

Nobody has presented any evidence that the Iraqis now possess weapons of mass destruction or the effective means, such as ballistic missiles, to deliver such weapons over long distances. Senator Richard Lugar himself admits, "We haven't found the evidence." During the Gulf War, when the Iraqis were under ferocious attack, the Scud missiles they fired at Israel were equipped only with conventional explosives, not with the chemical or biological warheads that everybody feared Saddam might use. Why would he act more recklessly in the future, when not under attack, than he did during the massive attack on his country in 1991?

At the recent Senate hearings, Senator Lincoln Chafee identified the crucial issue when he said, "the key here is the existence of the threat. And there's some dispute."

But is there any genuine dispute? All that's been shown is that Saddam, like many other national leaders, is working to develop weapons of mass destruction, and even that part of the story has been spun out of proportion by the administration and its friends in the media. There's many a slip, especially in a small, impoverished country such as Iraq, between working to develop such weapons and succeeding in developing them as well as the effective means of delivering them against the United States—leaving aside the critical question of Iraqi motivation for such a suicidal attack.

The truth of the matter seems to be that the Bush administration, apparently for reasons of political expediency, is obsessed with defeating Saddam's regime. To achieve this desired end, it is eager to launch a gigantic attack on a country that the United States first devastated in 1991 and has been provoking with aggressive overflights of Iraqi territory and sponsorship of anti-Saddam factions and intriguers for more than a decade. It's almost as if the principal grievance of the Bush administration is sheer frustration, piqued perhaps by the president's yearning to vindicate his father by finishing the job that George H. W. Bush did not finish. Who knows? Given the manifestly shoddy case the administration has made for its proposed war, one can only fall back on speculation about its real motives.

In 1821, Secretary of State John Quincy Adams declared that this country "goes not abroad in search of monsters to destroy." Now, however, it seems that doing so, by means of aggressive "preemptive" attacks, is to be the U.S. government's official policy. If the American people accede to this policy, we will suffer the fate that Adams himself feared would ensue. "The fundamental maxims of [U.S] policy would insensibly change from liberty to force," he said. America "might become the dictatress of the world. She would be no longer the ruler of her own spirit."

28

Helplessly, We Await the Catastrophe Our Rulers Are Creating

I cannot stop thinking of 1939, when everyone could see the war coming, and no one, it seemed, could do anything to stop it. Contemplating the impending catastrophe, W. H. Auden wrote,

> In the nightmare of the dark
> All the dogs of Europe bark,
> And the living nations wait,
> Each sequestered in its hate;
> Intellectual disgrace
> Stares from every human face
> And the seas of pity lie
> Locked and frozen in each eye.
>
> ("In Memory of W. B. Yeats," 1939)

Today, the dogs of war are barking not in Europe, but in the District of Columbia, and again people are looking on helplessly as the tragedy unfolds. We see the disaster being designed and touted, we observe the intellectual disgrace staring from the faces of George W. Bush and his advisers, and we note the seas of pity lying locked and frozen in their eyes. Yet we can do nothing to prevent the makers of this coming calamity from carrying out the devastation.

I wonder if they ever lie awake at night and imagine the faces of the men, women, and children—people they do not know, people who do not know them and who cannot harm them—who will be dead soon, their bodies crushed, ripped, and burned by the force of U.S. munitions exploding in their streets, homes, shops, schools, and hospitals. Those bombs are smart, no doubt, but they are better at math than at morality. Even when they work as they are supposed to, they are not smart enough to discriminate between the innocent and the guilty as they detonate in a densely populated urban area such as Baghdad. Do Dick Cheney and Donald Rumsfeld sleep peacefully nowadays, or do they awake haunted by visions of the innocent strangers they are preparing to obliterate? Do they rise at midnight to wash their hands, only to find that they cannot cleanse the damned spot?

In Congress, the politicians declare their strong support for the president's new policy of global preemptive wars and, in particular, for his impending assault on the ailing, impoverished, nearly defenseless Iraqis. The legislators dare not oppose the president's plan, because then their electoral opponents would call their patriotism into question. Their patriotism, it seems, requires that they sacrifice their clear constitutional duty for the sake of campaign appearances. A deeper patriotism—an allegiance to the principles of the American republic—lies beyond their comprehension. In the name of a vulgar and superficial patriotism, they forsake all loyalty to the traditions that once made the United States a beacon of freedom rather than a world-ranging bully to be feared and loathed. Congress may posture and pretend, but it will do nothing substantial to exercise its constitutional authority to decide whether to commit the nation to war. Better to go along, to pass a vague, blank-check resolution. Later, if the war goes badly, the members can criticize it; if it goes well, they can take credit for supporting it; but in no event will they put themselves in a position to be held genuinely accountable.

So, with our supine and cowardly representatives unwilling to resist the chief executive's usurpations, "we the people" can only wait and watch as the president allows his strings to be pulled by people for whom war will be not the last resort, but the option they will exercise as soon as they perceive a threat, however modest, to their mastery of the world. The old boundaries have become irrelevant. No longer does the U.S. government content itself to rule over a vast continental domain. No longer does it find satisfaction merely in a Monroe Doctrine that proclaims its hegemony in the Western Hemisphere. No, our rulers have declared in sufficiently plain language, in their new "National Security Strategy of the United States," made public on September 20, that they intend to dominate the entire world. Some members of the political class speak openly of empire; others avoid the word but embrace the substance. Make no mistake, however: the American republic is no longer just sick unto death; it is stone-cold dead.

Although many ordinary Americans appear to have no quarrel with what is being done in their name, many others oppose this imperial impudence and the brutalities that express and sustain it. For the dissidents, the government has prepared a suitable reception. The TIPS informants are getting ready to report suspicions about them. The prison cells wait to receive more "material witnesses," "enemy combatants," and anyone accused, no matter how baselessly, of aiding or abetting alleged terrorists. For these unfortunates, no writ of habeas corpus will spoil the government's day; no defense lawyer's shadow will darken the doorway of its secret interrogations. As the president and Attorney General John Ashcroft have made clear, if you are not with the government, you are against it, and they have demonstrated already how far they are willing to go to deal with those who are against. Henceforth, thanks to the USA PATRIOT Act, all of us will be subject to closer surveillance. As we are ever more systematically monitored and regimented by our own government, even the elementary freedoms of movement, speech, and assembly will go by the board. In time, all of us will learn to keep quiet if we know what is good for us and our families.

We are told that the government's new policies, with their perpetual wars "to keep the peace," will bring us security, but they will not do so. Instead, the American empire's global violence will create a bottomless reservoir of vengeful terrorists. By insisting on poking its imperial stick into every hornet's nest on the planet, the U.S. government will ensure that Americans will continue to be stung. Wherever they may travel, at home or abroad, they will be at risk of attack by aggrieved men and women.

Perhaps we should not weep. Maybe a once-free people who surrenders its liberties so readily, so unjustifiably, deserves nothing better. Meanwhile, we can only wait helplessly for our masters to commence the catastrophe in Iraq and heaven only knows where else.

29

To Make War, Presidents Lie

When American presidents prepare for foreign wars, they lie. Surveying our history, we see a clear pattern. Since the end of the nineteenth century, if not earlier, presidents have misled the public about their motives and their intentions in going to war. The enormous losses of life, property, and liberty that Americans have sustained in wars have occurred in large part because of the public's unwarranted trust in what their leaders told them before leading them into war.

In 1898, President William McKinley, having been goaded by muscle-flexing advisers and jingoistic journalists to make war on Spain, sought divine guidance as to how he should deal with the Spanish possessions, especially the Philippines, that U.S. forces had seized in what ambassador John Hay famously described as a "splendid little war." Evidently, his prayer was answered, because the president later reported that he had heard "the voice of God," and "there was nothing left for us to do but take them all and educate the Filipinos, and uplift and Christianize them."

In truth, McKinley's motivations had little if anything to do with uplifting the people whom William H. Taft, the first governor-general of the Philippines, called "our little brown brothers," but much to do with the political and commercial ambitions of influential expansionists such as Captain Alfred T. Mahan, Theodore Roosevelt, Henry Cabot Lodge, and their ilk. In short, the official apology for the brutal and unnecessary Philippine-American War was a mendacious gloss.

The Catholic Filipinos evidently did not yearn to be "Christianized" in the American style, at the point of a Krag rifle, and they resisted the U.S. imperialists as they had previously resisted the Spanish imperialists. The Philippine-American War, which officially ended on July 4, 1902, but actually dragged on for many years in some islands, cost the lives of more than 4,000 U.S. troops, more than 20,000 Filipino fighters, and more than 220,000 Filipino civilians, many of whom perished in concentration camps eerily similar to the relocation camps into which U.S. forces herded Vietnamese peasants some sixty years later.

When World War I began in 1914, President Woodrow Wilson's sympathies clearly lay with the British. Nevertheless, he quickly proclaimed U.S. neutrality and urged his fellow Americans to be impartial in both thought and deed. Wilson himself, however, leaned more and more toward the Allied side as the war proceeded. Still, he recognized that the great majority of Americans wanted no part of the fighting in Europe, and in 1916 he sought reelection successfully on the appealing slogan "He Kept Us Out of War."

Soon after his second inauguration, however, he asked Congress for a declaration of war, which was approved, although six senators and fifty members of the House of Representatives had the wit or wisdom to vote against it. Wilson promised this war would be "the war to end all wars," but wars aplenty have taken place since the guns fell silent in 1918, leaving their unprecedented carnage—nearly 9 million dead and more than 20 million wounded, many of them hideously disfigured or crippled for life, as well as perhaps 10 million civilians who died of starvation or disease as a result of the war's destruction of resources and its interruption of commerce. And what did the United States or the world gain? Only a twenty-year reprieve before the war's smoldering embers burst into flame again.

After World War I, Americans felt betrayed, and they resolved never to make the same mistake again. Yet, just two decades later, President Franklin D. Roosevelt began the maneuvers by which he hoped to plunge the nation once again into the European cauldron. Unsuccessful in his naval provocations of the Germans in the Atlantic, he eventually pushed the Japanese to the wall by a series of hostile economic-warfare measures, issued clearly unacceptable ultimatums, and induced them to mount a desperate military attack, most devastatingly on the U.S. forces he concentrated at Pearl Harbor.

Campaigning for reelection in Boston on October 30, 1940, FDR had sworn: "I have said this before, but I shall say it again and again: Your boys are not going to be sent into any foreign wars." Well, Peleliu ain't Peoria. Roosevelt was lying when he made his declaration, just as he had lied repeatedly before and would lie repeatedly for the remainder of his life. (Stanford University historian David M. Kennedy, careful not to speak too stridently, refers to FDR's "frequently cagey misrepresentations to the American public.") Yet many, many Americans trusted this inveterate liar, sad to say, with their lives, and during the war more than four hundred thousand of them paid the ultimate price.

Among FDR's many political acolytes was a young congressman, Lyndon Baines Johnson, who eventually and for the world unfortunately clawed his way to the presidency. As chief executive, he had to deal with vital questions of war and peace, and like his beloved mentor, he relied heavily on lying to the public. In October 1964, seeking to gain election by portraying himself as the peace candidate (in contrast to the alleged mad bomber Barry Goldwater), LBJ told a crowd at Akron University: "We are not about to send American boys nine or ten thousand miles away from home to do what Asian boys ought to be doing for themselves."

In 1965, however, shortly after the start of his elected term in office, Johnson exploited the Gulf of Tonkin Resolution, itself based on a fictitious account of attacks on U.S. naval forces off Vietnam, and initiated a huge buildup of U.S. forces in Southeast Asia that would eventually commit more than five hundred thousand American "boys" to fight an "Asian boy's" war. Some fifty-eight thousand U.S. military personnel would lose their lives in the service of LBJ's vanity and political ambitions, not to speak of the millions of Vietnamese, Cambodians, and Laotians killed and wounded in the melee. Chalk up another catastrophe to a lying American president.

Now President George W. Bush is telling the American people that we stand in mortal peril of imminent attack by Iraqis or their agents armed with weapons of mass destruction. Having presented no credible evidence or compelling argument for his characterization of the alleged threat, he simply invites us to trust him and therefore to support him as he undertakes what once would have been called naked aggression. Well, David Hume long ago argued that just because every swan we've seen was white, we cannot be certain that no black swan exists. So Bush may be telling the truth. In the light of history, however, we would be making a long-odds bet to believe him.

30

Saddam Hussein Can't Blackmail Us with a Fissionable Softball

In his speech at Cincinnati on October 7, President George W. Bush, seeking to rally support for his authorization to launch a military invasion of Iraq, portrayed the threat posed by the Iraqi regime in lurid terms. The Iraqis, he asserted, possess dreaded chemical and biological "weapons of mass destruction," and they seek to develop a nuclear weapon. "If the Iraqi regime is able to produce, buy, or steal an amount of highly enriched uranium a little larger than a single softball," the president warned, "it could have a nuclear weapon in less than a year." And then? "Saddam Hussein would be in a position to blackmail anyone who opposes his aggression. He would be in a position to dominate the Middle East. He would be in a position to threaten America."

Bush urged that "we cannot wait for the final proof—the smoking gun—that could come in the form of a mushroom cloud." Reiterating that Saddam can "develop a nuclear weapon to blackmail the world," the president opined that "the situation could hardly get worse" and therefore that the United States must eliminate the grave Iraqi threat before it comes to fruition.

This view of the world is so grotesquely out of proportion, so preposterously hyperbolic, that one scarcely knows what to make of it. The president, along with all those who find his presentation compelling, seems to have forgotten everything about the long Cold War, and he seems oblivious to nearly everything about the current world situation.

For some forty years, the United States lived under constant threat of nuclear attack by the Soviet Union. For those who have forgotten, the Soviet regime was not composed of poets and flower peddlers. If Saddam Hussein is, as the president insists, "a ruthless and aggressive dictator," what was Joseph Stalin? What was Leonid Brezhnev?

Nor did the rulers of the USSR play single softball with respect to nuclear warheads. By the mid-1980s, the Soviet arsenal contained more than ten thousand strategic nuclear warheads and some thirty thousand nonstrategic nuclear warheads. Unlike Iraq, which has no capability to deliver a nuclear weapon at long range, the USSR had more than six thousand nuclear warheads mounted on more than a thousand intercontinental ballistic missiles, most of them programmed to strike targets in the United States within half an hour of launch. In addition, thousands of submarine-launched nuclear weapons and more than a thousand nuclear bombs carried by long-range jet aircraft augmented the Soviet threat.

Yet, notwithstanding the tens of thousands of Soviet nuclear warheads and their sophisticated delivery vehicles kept in constant readiness, the United States was not "blackmailed" by the USSR. Odd that now the United States should quake at the prospect of a single Iraqi softball of fissionable material.

The United States itself, of course, created an awesome nuclear arsenal (not to speak of its vast stocks of chemical and biological weapons). Even today, after substantial post–Cold War cutbacks, the U.S. nuclear arsenal contains more than three thousand strategic nuclear warheads and thousands of nonstrategic nuclear weapons. Given that the United States is the only country ever to have used nuclear weapons in warfare, its willingness to use such weapons cannot be doubted.

Whereas Saddam Hussein has never threatened to use nuclear weapons against the United States, the United States has threatened to use such weapons against Iraq, most notably when President George H. W. Bush sent a letter to Saddam Hussein in January 1991, warning him against using chemical or biological weapons to fight the U.S. and other forces about to attack Iraq and not so subtly suggesting that nuclear retaliation might ensue if he did.

The Iraqi dictator was deterred in 1991; he can be deterred just as well in 2002 or in any future year. He understands fully that any use of weapons of mass destruction—suitcase nukes, deadly germs, nerve gas, or anything else—by him or any agent of his against the United States will elicit his immediate destruction, most likely by means of U.S. nuclear retaliation. Nothing in his history suggests that he is suicidal; on the contrary, he works extraordinarily hard at personal survival.

If the Iraqis understand the nuclear threat they face from the Americans, other regimes now understand that they too might become targets. According to the Bush administration's secret *Nuclear Posture Review* provided to Congress by Defense Secretary Donald Rumsfeld in January 2002, a partial copy of which was obtained by the *Los Angeles Times,* "The Bush administration has directed the military to prepare contingency plans to use nuclear weapons against at least seven countries [China, Russia, Iraq, North Korea, Iran, Libya, and Syria] and to build smaller nuclear weapons for use in certain battlefield situations." Leaders around the world have taken note of the new U.S. nuclear posture. They surely understand that although the United States does not speak softly, it does carry a big stick.

Clearly, then, given the constellation of forces and the understandings of all the parties regarding action and reaction, Iraq poses no nuclear threat to the American people or anyone else. President Bush's hyperventilation about the "mushroom cloud" is nothing but hot air, intended to inspire fear where such fear has no rational basis.

Unfortunately, we cannot say the same about nuclear threats from other quarters. The continuing existence of vast nuclear-weapons stockpiles and delivery systems in Russia constitutes a tremendous threat to the safety of humankind. Even if the Russians resist the deliberate employment of those weapons, the likelihood of accidental launches or catastrophic failures of their command-and-control system remains far from trivial. If President Bush really wanted to do something to allay the nuclear threat to the American people, he would put the full weight of his administration behind the most expeditious dismantling of as many of the Russian weapons as possible. The $1 billion a year the United States is spending currently to improve the security of Russian nuclear storage facilities is pathetically slight in proportion to the seriousness of the threat those ill-secured facilities pose to the world.

Also significant, though seldom mentioned by the establishment media, are the more than one hundred nuclear warheads believed to be in the Israeli arsenal. Little imagination is required to conceive of the targets the Israelis probably have in mind for those weapons. Bush seeks to inspire fear of nuclear attack in the residents of New York, Chicago, and San Francisco, but the residents of Baghdad and Damascus have far more reason to be afraid of finding themselves on the receiving end of such an attack.

Nor should we overlook the nuclear warheads and long-range missiles in the hands of the Pakistanis. Unlike Iraq, Pakistan has spawned, nurtured, and harbored countless thousands of Muslim holy warriors keen to harm the United States. Evidently, the Bush administration feels comfortable with Pakistani dictator General Pervez Musharraf because he is "our son of a bitch," but today's military strongman may be tomorrow's deposed dictator, and nobody knows how friendly toward the United States the replacement son of a bitch will be. A hostile, nuclear-armed Islamist regime in Pakistan might make the Taliban look like cute kindergarteners.

In sum, a nuclear threat does exist—in fact, several of them do—but the mythical softball in Baghdad is not among them. That President Bush and his warmongering advisers are hell-bent to invade Iraq is all too clear. That Iraq's nuclear program justifies such an invasion is the sheerest nonsense.

31

Why the Rush to War?

In the face of worldwide opposition to and growing domestic condemnation of the Bush administration's rush to war, the president has launched a new public-relations offensive to convince the world abroad and the American people that nothing can stop the United States from carrying out its impending military conquest of Iraq. In public appearances, the commander in chief has displayed ever more impatience not only with the Iraqi regime's actions, but also with anyone's even questioning his war policy. Merely repeating tired declarations that Saddam has brutalized his own people and "failed to disarm," President Bush has added nothing of substance to the administration's case for going to war. Instead, he has become petulant when asked to explain, for example, why he is so angrily intent on military action against Iraq while he is so serenely content to let diplomacy continue indefinitely to resolve the more serious threat posed by North Korea's barbarous regime.

None of the major European countries, save Great Britain, wants anything to do with a U.S. war against Iraq, and even Tony Blair's government, ordinarily subservient to U.S. wishes, recently has expressed a preference to let the inspections in Iraq continue, perhaps for months, before deciding whether to launch an invasion. The British people remain overwhelmingly opposed to the war, which must give the Labour chieftains pause as they contemplate the repercussions their present bellicosity may have on their candidates at the next election.

In the Middle East, opposition is similarly almost unanimous. Even the Turks, who normally allow themselves to be bought off fairly cheaply, are digging in their heels this time, fearful not only of the harm a war will wreak on their fragile economy, but also of the Kurdish thorn in their soft southern underbelly, which a war might sharpen substantially. The Gulf sheikdoms take the U.S. money and run, of course, mindful that in view of the American armada standing offshore, they have no good alternative. The Saudis continue to urge avoidance of a war, but, placed in an untenable position by U.S. diplomatic and economic pressures, they have reluctantly conceded a modicum of cooperation. Only Israel wishes the United States Godspeed in its attack on Iraq.

This pattern might well give Americans reason to rethink the Bush administration's policy. The president maintains that Iraq's regime poses a grave, imminent threat. Yet, if so, why do the countries that confront the alleged threat at closest range display no fear of Iraqi action against them? And if Israel alone is cheering for this war, what might that fact suggest? Well might we consider whether the present U.S. war policy constitutes still another case of the American dog being wagged by the tail of its Israeli protectorate. If so, do the American people really want a war?

For many months, administration officials have continued to make the same claims about Iraqi programs to produce and deploy so-called weapons of mass destruction, yet they have consistently refused to adduce clear evidence to back up their charges. Even after the UN inspectors returned to Iraq, the United States refused to make its intelligence data available to them. Is it really more important to preserve the details of the government's intelligence sources than to avert war by assisting the inspectors in locating and destroying the alleged Iraqi weapons, raw materials, and production facilities? If the U.S. government truly knows that such things exist in Iraq, what is so complicated about simply telling the inspectors where to find them? Not everything at issue can be hauled away on trucks as inspectors approach. On closer consideration, one begins to suspect that in fact the U.S. government's spooks do not have the information they claim to possess. Perhaps their knowledge consists of little more than scattered, unreliable reports and questionable inferences, held together by a glue of preconceptions. Maybe their intelligence is just as bad as U.S. intelligence about the USSR is now seen to have been during the Cold War.

In any event, the president's recently displayed impatience and undisguised hostility ill suit a leader who, thanks to congressional abdication, holds the power of war and peace in his own hands. War is too serious a matter to be decided by someone who lacks the keen intelligence and mature judgment to understand the situation fully and to weigh the pros and cons of alternative policies wisely. George Bush is doing nothing to reassure the public that he has what it takes to be a responsible foreign policymaker.

Worse, he appears to be acting under the greatest sway of advisers—Cheney, Rumsfeld, Wolfowitz, Perle, and their ilk—who have long been obsessed with attacking Iraq no matter what Saddam might do to placate them and who manifest a megalomania for remaking the Middle East in their preferred image. Their fantasies of transforming Iraq into a liberal democracy abide light years away from any realizable reality: Iraq lacks all the ingredients for baking that cake. If Americans allow themselves to become lodged in Iraq, ruling it directly or through a puppet regime, they will soon rue the day they plunged into that oil-rich but politically hopeless quagmire. If U.S. occupiers cannot deal successfully even with the rag-tag clans and warlords of Afghanistan, they won't stand a chance in the treacherous ethnic, religious, and political cauldron known as Iraq.

Ultimately, the most troubling aspect of the administration's present rush to war is its failure to treat the question of war and peace as the grave issue that it is. War consists of many horrors, most of them spilling onto wholly innocent parties. It ought never to be entered into lightly. Indeed, it ought always to be undertaken only after every decent alternative has been exhausted. We are far from having exhausted every good alternative. To allow more time for the inspections to proceed promises a far better ratio of benefits to costs than going straight to war.

That the United States already has positioned scores of thousands of troops near Iraq, ready to launch an attack, in no way justifies proceeding with that attack. Acting on a "use 'em or lose 'em" assumption makes no sense. Better to withdraw those forces than to commit them to a war that easily might have been avoided. The men and women in the U.S. armed forces certainly deserve to be kept out of harm's way unless a completely compelling reason exists to place their lives at risk. Nor do the countless Iraqi civilians who will suffer in any war deserve the harms that a U.S. attack will bring them. The ordinary Iraqi citizen is not the Iraqi regime. No defensible moral calculus can justify killing those hapless people—military conscripts as well as civilians—just because the Bush administration harbors an animus toward Saddam Hussein and his lieutenants.

Despite what President Bush insists, time is on our side, not Saddam's. We hold the upper hand in every way. It is no answer to catalog how under a host of conditions not yet realized and not likely to be realized soon the Iraqi regime someday might seriously harm the American people here on our own territory. Justification of war requires that we face a definite, immediate, grave threat, and the administration has put forth no evidence that Iraq poses such a threat to us. In the present circumstances, then, a U.S. attack on Iraq would constitute a clear, utterly unjustified act of aggression. We ought not to tolerate a government that commits such acts in our name.

32

Paul Craig Roberts Interviews Robert Higgs on War and Liberty

Paul Craig Roberts interviews Robert Higgs, senior fellow at the Independent Institute and author of Crisis and Leviathan, *a study of how war and crisis lead to the growth of government and the decline in liberty, about the unintended consequences of a possible American invasion of Iraq.*

PAUL CRAIG ROBERTS: Why do you oppose the Bush administration's policy toward Iraq?

ROBERT HIGGS: I oppose it on both moral and practical grounds. A "preemptive" war against Iraq entails a variety of morally indefensible actions, but even Americans who do not admit or cannot see its immorality will ultimately find its consequences intensely unpleasant.

PCR: Isn't it desirable to overthrow a brutal dictator?

RH: The world is rife with brutal regimes. If we hadn't been forewarned, we might have thought the president in his State of the Union speech was describing the tortures used in Turkey or Pakistan or Egypt. Yet the administration has no qualms about joining hands with these (and other) odious regimes. Worse, it is showering them with tens of billions of dollars extracted from American taxpayers. The United States cannot rid the world of all its brutal dictators, and even if it somehow managed to do so, new ones would pop up soon afterward. We ought to decline the fool's errand of perpetually enforcing our political standards on the entire world.

PCR: Isn't it a good idea to get rid of Saddam Hussein in particular?

RH: The world probably would be a better place without Saddam in power, but we have no assurance that a post-Saddam regime will be flush with sweetness and light. In view of Iraq's history, we have good reason to expect a regime more like the autocracies that have long prevailed there. The notion current in certain circles that Iraq is a democratic success waiting to happen is sheer nonsense. With its violent ethnic, religious, and political conflicts, Iraq may be incapable of cohering as anything other than a dictatorship. Nor will conducting some phony-baloney elections alter this situation; it will only put a pleasing ceremonial gloss on the ugly underlying realities.

PCR: What about the claim that the United States created successful democratic regimes as a result of its triumph in World War II?

RH: The analogy between postwar Germany or Japan and present-day Iraq is much too loose to be taken seriously. Among other things, our occupations and the reforms we imposed on Germany and Japan took place in a completely different geopolitical context. If the United States takes over Iraq, it certainly will inflame Muslim zealots all over the world, who will point to our conquest as proof certain of our evil intentions toward Muslims who have the temerity to challenge our hegemony. Nearby regimes in the region may be overthrown by factions angered by their governments' unwillingness to stand up to the Western crusaders. What good will it do to control Iraq if, for example, Saudi Arabia falls under the control of Islamic fanatics?

PCR: From your extensive research into previous U.S. wars, have you drawn any conclusions that shape your thinking about the present situation?

RH: One conclusion stands out: from the Civil War onward, engagement in war has left Americans less free when the war was over than they had been before the war. In countless ways, the warfare state has proved inimical to the preservation of liberty, just as patriots such as James Madison warned us long ago that it would. War brings higher taxes; greater government debt; increased government intrusion in markets; more pervasive government surveillance, manipulation, and control of the public. Going to war is the perfect recipe for expanding the size, scope, and power of the federal government. You have to wonder why so many conservatives, who claim to cherish liberty, enthusiastically embrace the government's schemes for plunging the nation into war.

PCR: Many claim that whatever war's risks to civil and economic liberties, it still generates definite economic benefits.

RH: That claim represents a prime example of what sound economists call the broken-window fallacy. Despite many current myths about so-called war prosperity, war is always an economic disaster. The resources used for war purposes cannot be used for alternative purposes; there's no free lunch, and the Keynesian arguments that imply one are just bad economics. I have spent years demonstrating that even World War II, which allegedly rescued the economy from the Great Depression, did nothing of the sort. Participation in the war simply substituted one kind of economic privation—a worse kind—for another. Genuine prosperity resumed only after the war ended.

PCR: Will a U.S. conquest of Iraq make us safer?

RH: No. It will probably increase the risk of terrorism for Americans both at home and abroad.

Paul Craig Roberts is the author, with Lawrence M. Stratton, of The Tyranny of Good Intentions: How Prosecutors and Bureaucrats Are Trampling the Constitution in the Name of Justice. *Reprinted by permission of Paul Craig Roberts and Creators Syndicate, Inc.*

33

Nuke France

Before I explain why it is imperative that President Bush nuke France, I should make clear that I harbor no ill will whatsoever toward the French. Indeed, some of my dearest friends are French, and I will be deeply saddened to bid them adieu. But it's got to be done. The real puzzle is why the Bush administration is taking so long to appreciate the gravity of the threat that France poses to U.S. national security.

For some time, the administration's Hitler *du jour* has been Saddam Hussein. Although Saddam is certainly no mother's little angel, the threat he constitutes to the American people has been greatly exaggerated, whereas the menace posed by the diabolical Jacques Chirac has gone nearly undetected until recently. Certain parallels, of course, have been too obvious to escape notice: both of these heads of state, for example, operate from palaces, although the Elysee Palace undoubtedly outshines the *gauche* edifices that Saddam inhabits.

Only in the past few weeks have FBI and CIA sleuths combined their data banks to discover that Chirac's activities as a dedicated anti-American terrorist began half a century ago when he disguised himself as a student and ordinary worker in order to gain access to the critical Anheuser-Busch facility in St. Louis, where he posed as a forklift operator, and to a highly classified Howard Johnson's, where, serving as a soda jerk, he was able to scope out U.S. stocks of carbon dioxide and other noxious chemicals in our weapons of mass destruction (WMDs) arsenal. Since those days of working as a member of a Gaullist cell hidden deep within the vast recesses in our all-too-welcoming country, he has continued to strive relentlessly to augment his power, his single goal being the complete domination of the United States and the subjection of its freedom-loving, English-speaking people to French lessons and *haute cuisine.*

Unlike Saddam, who worked in harmony with U.S. officials for many years prior to 1991 and expressed only pacific inclinations toward this country, Chirac has always insisted insanely on putting the interests of France above those of the United States. Nor has he kept his bellicosity under tight wraps. Only a few days ago, in an exclusive interview given to reporters for *Time,* the iron-fisted tyrant known in his own country as "Le Bulldozer" said, "France is not a pacifist country." Few could miss the implied threat to U.S. security in that naked declaration. Nor could anyone mistake his hostile intentions when he declared: "Regarding America's role as a sole superpower: Any community with only one dominant power is always a dangerous one, and provokes reactions."

Unlike Iraq, which lacks effective capacity to deliver WMDs to the United States even if it possessed them, France has not only developed a panoply of such devastating weapons, but built and deployed high-tech missiles, aircraft, surface vessels, and submarines to deliver warheads powerful enough to wreak unimaginable destruction on the United States. According to the *Bulletin of the Atomic Scientists* (July–August 2001), French spending for nuclear forces has been running at 15.8 billion francs ($2.3 billion) per year, roughly equivalent to 40 percent the entire gross domestic product of Iraq. Each of the French *Triomphant*-class submarines—note well the intimidating name—carries sixteen M45 submarine-launched ballistic missiles (SLBMs), each missile with six TN 75 nuclear warheads. France is developing a new SLBM, the M51, which will replace the M45, carry as many as six warheads each, and possess a range of eight to ten thousand kilometers (in contrast to Iraq's ridiculous Scuds, which are little more than flying tin cans of limited range and highly dubious accuracy). With its inventory of 288 nuclear warheads for its SLBMs, 50 for its Mirage 2000N bombers, and 10 for its carrier-based Super Etendard aircraft, France is effectively positioned to blackmail the United States and the world unless George Bush exercises the fortitude required to knock out this potentially catastrophic threat before the pitiless Chirac unleashes it on unsuspecting Americans.

Lest anyone doubt the capacity of the cold-hearted French supreme leader to use his nuclear weapons against the United States, we would do well to recall how he defied world opinion in 1995 when he carried out nuclear tests at Mururoa Atoll in the South Pacific, provoking Australian acting prime minister Kim Beazley to characterize Chirac's actions as evincing "an arrogant disregard" for the UN General Assembly resolution demanding a halt to the tests. Saddam Hussein has submitted to UN conditions and admitted scores of UN inspectors to verify that he has no WMDs. Jacques Chirac, however, continues to defy world opinion and to maintain a nuclear arsenal primed to destroy anyone who obstructs his ambition to dominate first Europe and then, of course, the entire world.

Unlike the chickenhawks who occupy the higher reaches of the Bush administration, Chirac is a battle-hardened soldier who fought and was wounded in the brutal Algerian conflict during the 1950s. If that experience itself does not demonstrate sufficiently the ice water in his veins, one might bear in mind that he also graduated from the École Nationale d'Administration, the elite training academy for Europe's cruelest bureaucrats. Clearly, he is a man who will stop at nothing.

Thus, the gauntlet has been thrown down. All that remains is to see whether George W. Bush will accept the challenge. Will Bush understand that whereas Iraq might well be left to rot away for years before requiring serious U.S. attention, France constitutes at this very instant a monstrous threat—a danger that can only be described as *massif*—to all Americans and their way of life, especially their indulgence in fast food and their near-total ignorance of *la gloire de la France?* Against Iraq, a U.S. attack might be, at best, preventive; against France, in stark contrast, a U.S. attack would be, without a doubt, preemptive. The Franco-threat is real: the steely-eyed Chirac has the means, and he has the motive. Will George Bush do what must be done, or, for us Américains, will this be *la fin?*

PART VII

Slaughtering the Innocent

34

Collateral Damage
Two Venues, One Logic

Timothy McVeigh, it is fair to say, will go down in history as a terrorist. He set off a bomb that killed innocent men, women, and children along with the government agents against whom he had decided to retaliate for their assaults on Americans at Waco and elsewhere. In a letter sent to Gore Vidal, dated April 4, 2001, McVeigh described the reasons for his action:

> When an aggressor force continually launches attacks from a particular base of operations, it is sound military strategy to take the fight to the enemy. Additionally, borrowing a page from U.S. foreign policy, I decided to send a message to a government that was becoming increasingly hostile, by bombing a government building and the government employees within that building who represent that government. Bombing the Murrah Federal Building was morally and strategically equivalent to the U.S. hitting a government building in Serbia, Iraq, or other nations. Based on observations of the policies of my own government, I viewed this action as an acceptable option. From this perspective what occurred in Oklahoma City was no different than what Americans rain on the heads of others all the time, and, subsequently, my mindset was and is one of clinical detachment. (reproduced in Gore Vidal, "The Meaning of Timothy McVeigh," *Vanity Fair,* September 2001, p. 410)

Last fall, in the wake of the September 11 attacks on the World Trade Center and the Pentagon, the U.S. government launched its so-called war on terrorism, aiming first to destroy al Qaeda and that organization's Taliban enablers in Afghanistan. Much of the U.S. military action in Afghanistan has taken the form of bombing and other aerial attacks on supposed enemy personnel, structures, and

Originally appeared April 18, 2002

equipment. The situation on the ground, however, has proven to be less than transparent: it has been difficult to distinguish friend from foe, innocuous civilian from armed fighter.

Army Special Forces Team 555, among others, undertook the task of identifying enemy personnel and property and directing aerial attacks on them. When U.S. military pilots expressed misgivings about attacking particular targets, the team's leader, Chief Warrant Officer Dave Diaz, opted to "play this terminology game." He told his men: "Yes, it is a civilian village, mud hut, like everything else in this country. But don't say that. Say it's a military compound. It's a built-up area, barracks, command and control. Just like with the convoys: If it really was a convoy with civilian vehicles they were using for transport, we would just say hey, military convoy, troop transport" (qtd. in Dana Priest, "U.S. Had Difficulty Identifying Targets," *New Orleans Times-Picayune,* February 20, 2002, reprinted from the *Washington Post*). The pilots came to accept the judgments of the fire controller on the ground and directed their ordnance accordingly. Although Warrant Officer Diaz claims that his group attempted to avoid killing civilians, on certain occasions Team 555 members found women and children intermingled with persons they took to be Taliban fighters "they needed to strike at that moment." In those instances, "the guidance I gave my team, and the guidance from higher (headquarters), is that they are combatants" (qtd. in Priest, "U.S. Had Difficulty").

Elsewhere in Afghanistan, after an air strike in early March caused the death of a woman and the wounding of a child, a U.S. commander at Bagram Air Base said he had not known that the woman and the child were in the vehicle on which he had ordered the attack, but he also said that, had he known, he would not have changed his orders: "we would have gone ahead and attacked anyway" (qtd. in David Wood, "Status of Women, Children Questioned after Airstrike," *New Orleans Times-Picayune,* March 14, 2002). Some U.S. military officers questioned whether killing civilians was the best way to win the support of the local populace, but others expressed the view that the actions taken by al Qaeda had removed the need for moral niceties: "In a war to the bone like this one, where the enemy's immorality is publicly proven, if they involve their noncombatants then they become legitimate targets, no matter how regrettably" (qtd. in Wood, "Status of Women").

After U.S. ground troops had mistakenly attacked a group of Afghans who were not affiliated with the Taliban or al Qaeda, killing sixteen of them and taking twenty-seven others captive for a time and roughing them up before releasing them, Secretary of Defense Donald Rumsfeld declined to apologize: "Let's not call them 'innocents,'" he told reporters. "We don't know quite what they were. They were people who fired on our forces" (qtd. in Thom Shanker, "Attack Victims not Taliban or al-Qaida," *New Orleans Times-Picayune,* February 22, 2002, reprinted from the *New York Times*). Self-defense, it would appear, is not a valid excuse for firing on attacking U.S. troops. Rumsfeld declined to blame his forces for their actions and indicated that no disciplinary action would be taken against those responsible for carrying out the attack: "Why would there be? I can't imagine why there would be any" (qtd. in Shanker, "Attack Victims").

35

Military Precision versus
Moral Precision

Now that the long period of peace-seeking pretense has ended and George W. Bush has unleashed his dogs of war on Iraq, many of the questions that have occupied us during the past year have been dispatched by the fait accompli of the U.S. invasion. Even in the midst of war, however, certain questions remain relevant, and one of the most important pertains to precision—to hitting, so to speak, what one aims to hit.

Television viewers are being treated, if that is the right word, to much expert commentary by retired military officers and other experts on the conduct of war. A great deal of this commentary has to do with technology, and once again, as in 1991, the technology of modern warfare is receiving high praise. News people seem awestruck by the accounts of bombs and missiles that not only hit, say, a targeted building, but enter the third window on the second floor and strike the handle of the hot-water faucet on the basin in the washroom. Golly, General Turgidson, that's fantastic!

If the extreme accuracy being claimed for today's bombs and missiles were being considered only in relation to the munitions' purely military utility in demolishing the persons and property selected for destruction, we might let the matter pass without extended consideration, treating it as a topic of special interest only to those fascinated with the technology of death, but the people responsible for employing these instruments of war have themselves taken pains to connect their use with—of all things—morality.

Thus, Defense Secretary Donald Rumsfeld recently remarked on "the care . . . , the humanity that goes into" the use of so-called smart bombs and similar munitions. No doubt we should take note when the minister of war expresses solicitude for those who otherwise might be written off as "collateral damage." Still, amid the dazzling, often video-illustrated descriptions and accounts of the wonderful precision of these munitions, the reporters, the talking heads, and, one fears, the television viewers as well are losing sight of what, precisely, is going on.

To begin, one must distinguish between the precision with which a bomb or missile hits its intended point of impact—often claimed to be only a few meters most of the time—and the area within which lethal damage will be wreaked when the warhead explodes. In Iraq, for example, the much-used Joint Direct Attack Munition (JDAM), a two-thousand-pound Mark-84 dumb bomb with a global-positioning-system guidance kit attached to enhance its accuracy, is supposed to strike within 13 meters of its intended point of impact, as compared to an error range of some 60–70 meters for its dumb counterpart. Evidently, this difference is what elicited Rumsfeld's remark about the humanity of the use of such weapons: whereas the dumb bomb places at risk innocent souls 70 meters away, the smart one spares everybody beyond, say, 15 meters. If only it were so.

Recalling the hugely exaggerated claims made for precision bombing in past wars, we are entitled to skepticism even with respect to the accuracy claims themselves. According to some authorities, perhaps 7–10 percent of the smart bombs fall beyond the claimed accuracy radius—some of them miles away—because of mechanical and electrical malfunctions. The potential harm caused by a two-thousand-pound bomb hitting substantially off target in a city will be sufficiently obvious to anyone.

For purposes of the present discussion, however, let us concede that the bombs and missiles strike with all the accuracy claimed for them. What happens then? As described recently by Newhouse reporter David Wood, the two-thousand-pound JDAM "releases a crushing shock wave and showers jagged, white-hot metal fragments at supersonic speed, shattering concrete, shredding flesh, crushing cells, rupturing lungs, bursting sinus cavities and ripping away limbs in a maelstrom of destruction." Hardly anyone survives within 120 meters of the blast, where pressures of several thousand pounds per square inch and 8,500-degree heat simply obliterate everything, human and material. Metal fragments are spewed nearly three-quarters of a mile, and bigger pieces may fly twice that far; no one within 365 meters can expect to remain unharmed, and persons up to 1,000 meters or farther away from the point of impact may be harmed by flying fragments. Of course, the explosions also start fires over a wide area, which themselves may do vast damage, even to structures and people unharmed by the initial blast.

I am no munitions expert, but I am pretty good at basic math. Baghdad is a city of some 6,400,000 persons living in an area of approximately 734 square kilometers—roughly comparable to the urban areas of Boston or Detroit. If it were a perfect square it would be approximately 27 kilometers (17 miles) on a side, but the central, most densely populated part, where the prime military targets are concentrated, is a much smaller area. What are the odds that the damage wreaked by exploding two-thousand-pound JDAMs and other powerful munitions, such as the one-thousand-pound warheads on the Tomahawk missiles, will not touch the ordinary people of the city? Well, the odds are zero. Such powerful warheads, which the U.S. forces are expending by the thousands, cause explosions whose effects undoubtedly reach vast numbers of the city's civilian inhabitants. To conclude otherwise, one would be obliged to deny either the well-advertised power of the weapons themselves or the axioms of geometry.

As Marc W. Herold has written, "along with the U.S. military planners' decision to bomb perceived military targets in urban areas, the use of weapons with great destructive blast and fragmentation power necessarily results in heavy civilian casualties." Which brings us back to the matter of morality.

Many people, unfortunately, will maintain that such "collateral damage" is simply an unfortunate side effect of modern warfare, and if we are satisfied that the war itself is justified, then we are obliged to swallow hard and accept, however regrettably, the deaths and destruction wreaked upon the innocent in the neighborhood of the selected military targets. Some, including President Bush, even go so far as to place the blame for such harms on Saddam Hussein, who stands accused of cynically employing his "own people" as shields and of exploiting their destruction for public-relations purposes. This argument is a curious defense of the bombing—after all, no bombing, no such collateral damage—and the whole world knows that nothing required the president to go to war against Iraq: if ever a war was freely chosen, this war is the one.

In truth, aerial bombardment of urban areas using powerful munitions is inherently undiscriminating. The reporters, retired generals, and talking heads can huff and puff as much as they like, but the reality is that dropping two-thousand-pound bombs in densely populated cities will certainly kill and wound many innocent people—men, women, and children.

How can those who choose to employ such weapons in such circumstances continue to argue against, say, the hijackers of September 11 on the grounds that those evil men chose to kill innocents? Killing innocents is killing innocents. To conduct warfare as the United States is now conducting it in Iraq is necessarily to indulge in immoral conduct. The imprecision with which this sort of warfare treats the guilty and the innocent, by simply disregarding their differences, cannot withstand moral scrutiny. It will not do to say that the United States could avoid harming the innocent only by refraining from carrying out the war and that the no-war option has been ruled out. Someone has ruled it out, and that person, George W. Bush, along with his subordinates carrying out his war of aerial bombardment all the way down the chain of command, has chosen to act immorally. We are not dealing with a gray area here. This kind of intrinsically indiscriminate killing is deeply, outrageously immoral.

36

Some Are Weeping, Some Are Not

For the sailors on the U.S. aircraft carriers steaming back to their home ports, the war is over, but for Mona Hassan it has just begun. Gesturing as if she were plucking out her own eyes, she wails, "I would take them and give them to my son." Hoarse with grief, she pleads, "Take my eyes, take them! Who can watch their child like this, and live?"

Mona is grieving for her five-year-old son Ali Mustafa Hassan, who lost both eyes when his three-year-old cousin Hassan Ali Hussein triggered an explosion by picking up a bomblet from a U.S. cluster bomb that had fallen into the garden outside their home in Baghdad. Now little Ali, swathed in bandages, lies wailing in a hospital bed, and Mona suffers inconsolably.

Mona Hassan is weeping, but George W. Bush is not.

Although the big military maneuvers have come to an end in Iraq, and some U.S. troops are being redeployed to prepare for the next regime change, the deaths and injuries continue in Iraq. Indeed, they will continue for many years, even if not another bomb is dropped, not another rocket or artillery shell is fired, because the United States has already sown the land with countless thousands of unexploded munitions, including vast numbers of bomblets like the one that blinded little Ali, and in due course they will take their grisly toll, mainly on the curious children who stumble across them.

Already, however, the invading U.S. forces have planted more than enough seeds to guarantee a bountiful harvest of sorrow.

Eleven-year-old Amer Mahmoud is among the many already victimized. He accidentally kicked a piece of unexploded ordnance as he walked through a field toward his home in outer Baghdad. The explosion ripped his leg to shreds, and the leg had to be amputated. "Everything in my life has changed," whispers Amer from his hospital bed. "I cannot see now what my future will be." Certainly much pain and probably a lifetime of desperate struggle await little Amer, and naturally he is afraid.

Amer Mahmoud's life is devastated, but Donald Rumsfeld's life is not.

Twenty-year-old Walid Hijazi may never sleep peacefully again. He will be haunted by the memory of how his baby sister Rawand died a hideous death in her father's arms after her legs were blown away by the explosion of a U.S. bomblet that family members had brought into their apartment, curious and ignorant of what is was. Rawand's aunt, Suha Jamal, says bitterly, "Rawand was the enemy of no American." Tell it to Dick Cheney, madam.

Walid Hijazi and Suha Jamal will find their sleep disturbed by horrifying nightmares, but Dick Cheney will not.

Khalid Tamimi and four other members of his family were walking on a footpath in Baghdad when his brother, seven-year-old Haithem, spotted something interesting, picked it up and examined it, then threw it down. The bomblet's explosion killed Haithem and his nine-year-old cousin Nora and seriously wounded Khalid, as well as Amal and Mayasa, the children's mothers.

Khalid, Amal, and Mayasa Tamimi are wounded and grief stricken, but Paul Wolfowitz is not.

Khessma Radi has been overcome with anguish. At the burial of her twenty-two-year-old son Hashim Kamel Radi, she staggered from the graveside, wailing and beating her chest. All day she continued to beat herself unless restrained by her sister or her daughter. Hashim, a student, had been killed by gunfire from U.S. aircraft while riding a bus home from Baghdad to Nasiriyah. "Our lives are full of fire and weeping," cries Hashim's cousin Hussain Urabi. "The United States is now doing the same as Saddam did, so how can we build civilization?" Ask Richard Perle, Mr. Urabi; he knows.

For Khessma Radi and Hussain Urabi, the future is grim, but for Richard Perle it is not.

By now the whole world knows about Ali Ismail Abbas. Twelve-year-old Ali was asleep in his home in Baghdad when a U.S. missile struck, and the explosion tore off both his arms and killed his parents and his brother. Lying in a hospital bed, terrified and crying, he asked a Reuters reporter, "Can you help get my arms back?" Well, Ali, you're asking the wrong person. You should be asking Colin Powell; he's very close to the seat of power in this world, so he just might be able to help.

Ali's life, such as remains of it, is shattered, but Colin Powell's life is not.

It has often been said that war is Hell, but the saying is only half right. In truth, it's Hell for some and perfectly splendid for others. For Mona Hassan, Amer Mahmoud, Walid Hijazi, Khalid Tamimi, Khessma Radi, Ali Ismail Abbas, and thousands of others like them, all perfectly innocent of threatening anybody, life now holds the prospect of endless misery, but for George W. Bush, Donald Rumsfeld, Dick Cheney, Paul Wolfowitz, Richard Perle, and Colin Powell, the powerful architects of that boundless suffering, the future looks bright.

37

Are Pro-war Libertarians Right?

My essay "Some Are Weeping, Some Are Not" is an invitation for people to face squarely some of the consequences of what the U.S. government has done in its invasion of Iraq. Evidently, my invitation touched a raw nerve in many people, because I have been receiving a good deal of hostile mail in regard to it. Setting aside all those who dismiss it (and me) on Neanderthal grounds, the thrust of this mail is in large part along the lines of the following:

> There were hundreds of thousands of Iraqis, including children, who were imprisoned, tortured, maimed, and killed by Saddam's regime. Further, such rights violations would've continued had his regime been allowed to continue. You can't ignore all this without rendering your arguments hollow.

In response, I would emphasize at the outset that it is wrong to take actions that kill and maim innocent people. Period. It's just wrong, whether one's ideological outlook be libertarian or anything else half civilized. The best face one might put on taking such actions is that by committing these wrongs, one prevents even greater wrongs. In the present case, making such a judgment with anything approaching well-grounded assurance calls for powers that none of us possesses.

How does anybody know, for example, what the future harms caused to innocent parties by Saddam and his henchmen would have been, or that those harms, somehow properly weighted and discounted, would be greater than the harms caused by the U.S. armed forces in their invasion of Iraq? Such judgments turn on both factual speculations and subjective weightings that are, at best, open to serious question. Here in the United States, far from the scene and subject to constant bombardment by government and media disinformation, people are extremely ill-placed to arrive at well-informed judgments about Iraq in any event.

How do we know that, now that the old Iraqi regime has been chased away, the harms supposedly prevented will not actually take place under a new regime? Have all the cruel people who populated Iraq in times past simply evaporated? I scarcely think so. It is entirely possible that new crimes will continue to be perpetrated against innocent parties in Iraq. In fact, I will bet on it with heavy odds. Moreover, the occupying U.S. forces already seem to have fallen into a pattern of shooting down members of crowds—some of them children—protesting the U.S. presence: thus, new wrongs continue to be piled atop the previous ones daily, and in all likelihood they will continue to be so piled for years to come. Odd, Saddam is gone, but not all is sweetness and light in Iraq.

Suppose, for purposes of argument, one conceded that removal of the old Iraqi regime was a moral action, all things being considered. From this assumption, it does not follow that any and all actions purportedly taken in the service of the ostensible goal are themselves morally unimpeachable. Scattering cluster bomblets about areas inhabited by civilians, for example, was inexcusable: doing so was in no way necessary to oust Saddam's government. Nor was the use of very high-explosive bombs (two thousand pounds and bigger) in densely populated urban areas a means one can defend morally. With but a modicum of thought, one can think of all sorts of ways in which the United States could have overthrown Saddam's regime without wreaking nearly so much harm to innocents. The government keeps telling us how careful and humane it has been in its military operations in Iraq, but this official line is contemptible propaganda. Nor should the government be excused for its crimes merely because other governments on other occasions have behaved even more egregiously (for example, the U.S. government in its first war against Iraq in 1991). The not-so-bad-as-Dresden-or-Nagasaki test is, shall we say, not a very exacting one.

For some people, the concession that the old Iraqi regime ought to have been removed is sufficient to justify everything done under the rubric of "making war." But uttering the incantation "war" does nothing to remove one's actions from applicable moral strictures. Whatever is wrong in peace is wrong in war. This maxim in no way constitutes a refusal to see that in wars "hard choices" must be made. Hard choices always must be made. Human beings have developed moral codes precisely because they need guidance in making such choices. When governments go to war, they want their subjects to set aside everything they have believed about morality and to substitute a slavish acceptance of whatever the government pronounces necessary in order to "win the war." I have been appalled to see how many libertarians, of all people, have fallen for this government manipulation during the past year and a half. Better than others, libertarians ought to appreciate that war has been the health of the state, including the U.S. state, and that all such wars constitute, directly and indirectly in countless ways, further steps toward our own continuing enslavement.

Finally, I would merely point out again that my essay sought also to vivify the contrast between the sufferings of the innocents in Iraq and the blessings now being enjoyed by Bush and company, who engineered these horrors. If the situation truly had been a tragic one in which great wrongs *had* to be done in order to prevent even greater wrongs, then the only humane sentiment to carry away from the event is one of profound sadness because, after all, no matter what the seeming justification, one *has* committed great wrongs. Bush, Rumsfeld, Cheney, and the rest of the gang, however, are not overcome with sorrow. They are now out yucking it up with the fat cats on the campaign trail. One needs to face these concrete realities; war is not about abstractions. Now that its first phase has ended, some human beings are mourning, but others are doing just dandy. People ought to think about that situation and about the fact that the doing-dandy crowd consists precisely of the people whose actions brought about the deaths and injuries for which others are mourning.

Yesterday morning's newspaper (May 1, 2003) quotes a statement made to reporters by Lieutenant General Jay Garner, the U.S. viceroy of Iraq, as follows: "You all are reporting a lot about some demonstrations, and yeah, there's some demonstrations. . . . [But] [d]amn, fellas, we ought to be beating our chests every morning. We ought to look in the mirror and get proud and suck in our bellies and stick out our chests and say, 'Damn, we're Americans,' and smile." In the circumstances, if this is not obscene, then obscenity does not exist.

38

Not Exactly an Eye for an Eye

In the attacks of September 11, 2001, Muslim terrorists killed some three thousand people, about 90 percent of them in the World Trade Center, the rest on the hijacked airliners and in the Pentagon. The taking of life shocked many people the world over, not the least of them the president of the United States. Regardless of one's ethical, religious or political beliefs, no one could condone the murder of thousands of innocent people.

In the "war on terrorism" that ensued, President Bush sought, or so he claimed, to "bring to justice" the responsible parties. The first difficulty, of course, was that the nineteen people most directly responsible for the crimes were already dead. Bush looked past them, however, in his quest to "root out" all those who might have harbored or otherwise aided the perpetrators. This project made some moral sense: we all understand the concept of "accomplice to murder."

At this juncture, however, the president's moral vision must have grown murky. The hijackers' main abettors were identified as members of a shadowy radical Islamic organization known as al Qaeda, whose principal training sites lay in Afghanistan. When the Taliban rulers of Afghanistan refused to hand over al Qaeda's leader, Osama bin Laden, in accordance with a U.S. ultimatum, the president loosed a military assault on Afghanistan, the major component of which consisted of heavy aerial bombardments in support of local anti-Taliban groups momentarily allied with the United States.

Although the Taliban was chased from power and dispersed into hiding places in the mountains and elsewhere, the U.S. bombardment took a substantial toll of innocent civilians. Estimates vary widely, and by the very nature of the situation they cannot be made very reliable or precise. Nonetheless, reports by a number of U.S. and foreign journalists and other observers on the ground indicate that during the first two months of the campaign—a campaign that continues today—at least one thousand and perhaps as many as four thousand civilians were killed. Since then, the toll has mounted as U.S. forces have continued to expend bombs, rockets, and other munitions on an assortment of targets ranging from mountain caves to inhabited villages to isolated automobiles. Professor Marc Herold of the University of New Hampshire calls his estimate of nearly thirty-eight hundred Afghan civilians killed between October 7 and December 7, 2001, "very, very conservative," although others regard his estimate as too large.

Thus, the president, setting out to "bring to justice" those who had aided or harbored the perpetrators of the September 11 attacks, has succeeded in adding the deaths of thousands of innocent Afghans to the toll of those killed by the hijackers in 2001. U.S. officials have consistently shrugged off these deaths; when they admit causing them at all, they designate them unintended "collateral damage" and therefore of no great significance. A morally clear-eyed view must regard them as gross injustices that only augment the initial crimes the president ostensibly sought to avenge.

The killings of innocent Afghans, however, now pale in comparison with the number of innocent people killed in the U.S. invasion and occupation of Iraq, a country whose leaders were never shown to have had anything to do with the September 11 attacks. On June 11, the Associated Press (AP) announced the results of its own survey, which is based on the records of 60 of Iraq's 124 hospitals as well as on interviews with hospital officials. It covers the period from March 20 to April 20, the time of the heaviest fighting.

Besides not surveying all of the country's hospitals, the AP found that death records were far from complete, in part because many of those killed were never taken to hospitals and were buried quickly by their families, and in part because some victims were buried under debris or obliterated by explosions. Still, the surveyors confirmed the deaths of at least 3,240 civilians. Other investigators have arrived at much greater figures. Douglas W. Cassel Jr., in the *Chicago Daily Law Bulletin* of May 29, reports that "human rights and humanitarian groups suggest a civilian death toll of somewhere between 5,000 and 10,000." Again, the range is plausible; no one will ever know the exact number.

If we take as reasonable lower-bound estimates two thousand Afghan and four thousand Iraqi civilian deaths, then we can conclude that the U.S. forces already have inflicted at least two undeserved deaths for every death the terrorists caused in the September 11 attacks. Many of the dead in Afghanistan and Iraq are women and children. Moreover, many of the thousands of Iraqi army personnel killed in the invasion arguably ought to be regarded as essentially innocent because as conscripts they were fighting only under duress (and only in defense of their homeland). Thus, in a grotesque mockery of justice, the Bush administration has taken several innocent lives for each innocent life lost at the hands of the terrorists.

One might say—as many do—that the two killing sprees are not comparable because the terrorists set out to kill the innocent, whereas the U. S. forces killed the innocent "by accident." I greatly doubt, however, that this argument can hold water. When U.S. forces employ aerial and artillery bombardment—with huge high-explosive bombs, large rockets and shells, including cluster munitions—as their principal technique of waging war, especially in densely inhabited areas, they know with absolute certainty that many innocent people will be killed. To proceed with such bombardment, therefore, is to choose to inflict those deaths.

If you or I settled our scores in our neighborhoods in such a fashion, neither moral authorities nor the legal system would countenance our slaughter of innocent bystanders as excusable. Nobody can gain moral absolution merely by labeling his killing spree a "war." It's not a morally valid way out for you and me, and it's not a morally valid way out for George W. Bush, either.

39

Defense of Your Home Is Not Terrorism, Not Even in Iraq

Although President George W. Bush declared the U.S. military conquest of Iraq a success more than two months ago, the killing continues on a daily basis, and so do U.S. government efforts to paint a smiling face on the death, destruction, and disorder its invasion has brought to the hapless Iraqi people. According to Bush and U.S. proconsul L. Paul Bremer III, life is returning to normal in Iraq, but if a lack of electrical power, basic sanitation, and public safety is normal, then the unfortunate Iraqis must be praying for the quick advent of abnormality.

Bush vows that the continuing attacks on U.S. troops in Iraq will not dissuade him from the "restoration" of the conquered country. He insists that the attackers consist only of hardcore Baathists and "terrorists." Against these holdouts, the U.S. military commander Lieutenant General David McKiernan promises to "strike hard and with lethal force" whenever and wherever the opportunity arises to crush the opponents of the U.S. occupation.

This official characterization of the situation on the ground, however, rings increasingly hollow. Even the casual reader of news reports has learned that the huge U.S. campaigns against alleged resisters—Operation Peninsula Strike, Operation Desert Scorpion, and most recently Operation Sidewinder—amount to ill-informed, indiscriminate efforts marked more by overwhelming military force and massive firepower than by genuine understanding of the actual situation. Equipped only with sledge hammers, the Americans are now trying to perform brain surgery, and they are not having much success.

How could it be otherwise? U.S. soldiers are neither trained nor inclined to act as police. They know nothing about how to investigate crime, identify proper suspects, and apprehend them without wreaking enormous harm on innocent bystanders. In Iraq, the Americans operate under the tremendous handicap of not understanding either the language or the customs of the people they seek to control. Nor are the U.S. troops a corps of architects, construction engineers, public-health experts, and social workers. They are trained killers. To expect them to "reconstruct" Iraq is silly. The army's job is to destroy, not to build.

Placed in an untenable position, the troops now patrol Iraqi cities and maintain checkpoints on the streets, making themselves targets of opportunity for any Iraqi who chooses to attack them. Obviously, Iraq is flush with military rifles, rocket-propelled grenades, and other weapons, and with men trained to use them. In this hostile and dangerous situation, U.S. troops naturally get itchy trigger fingers. Sweltering miserably in their body armor, they become more inclined, as *New York Times* reporter Edmund L. Andrews reported on July 2, "to shoot first and ask questions later."

Andrews also noted that the frequent U.S. shootings and other assaults on Iraqis are "leaving a trail of bitterness, confusion and hunger for revenge." How could they fail to do so? In recent incidents, a multitude of innocent people have been mistakenly targeted, hit by stray bullets, and harmed by explosions and fires. In a village north of Baghdad, for example, a family of shepherds was shot by U.S. tanks. Elsewhere, a family was killed while working to extinguish fires that U.S. flares had started in a wheat field.

Traffic checkpoints in the cities provide venues for recurrent incidents of trigger-happy soldiers loosing their firepower on—well, who's to say who the targeted persons are? U.S. Army Major Scott Slaten, a public-affairs officer, declares that the drivers running checkpoints are "usually criminals, Baathists, or people fleeing crimes who didn't think they would get caught," but how can the frightened young corporal at a checkpoint possibly know the character or intentions of the driver he guns down in an instant reaction?

We're not exactly dealing with due process when a nervous soldier lets loose a burst from a heavy machine gun, as one did recently in a Baghdad incident that an Iraqi witness described by saying, "They killed innocent people for nothing." Witnesses said no signs ordered drivers to stop, and drivers easily might have missed or misunderstood the soldiers who waved them down from the roadside. In another recent checkpoint incident, witnesses said the car had stopped before a U.S. soldier fired on it with a heavy machine gun, wounding its elderly driver as well as the occupants of a nearby vehicle hit by stray bullets. Machine guns and densely occupied urban areas make a lethal combination.

Americans puzzled by why conditions won't settle down in Iraq seem mesmerized by official U.S. propaganda depicting the conquest and occupation of the country as a "liberation." To solve this puzzle, we need only to turn the situation around in our own minds. Imagine that the Iraqi army now controls your town. Imagine that from time to time for no apparent reason, they burst into homes, kicking, clubbing, and shooting the occupants and hauling some off as captives to unknown destinations. Imagine that the Iraqis passing by your home train their tank cannons on it, that the Iraqis on the streets aim their automatic rifles at you and your children as you go about your shopping. Imagine that from time to time they shoot a twelve-year-old child foolish enough to peer at them at the wrong time in the wrong place. Imagine that when you and your neighbors peacefully protest their actions, they sometimes fire wildly into the crowd of demonstrators and the adjacent buildings. Think about all these sorts of horrors, which now compose day-to-day life for the Iraqi people, and put yourself in their place.

Then ask yourself: When you choose to fight back against the foreigners' brutal occupation of your country, your city, and your neighborhood, to resist the desecration of your place of worship, to seek revenge for the arbitrary slaughter of your loved ones, does anyone have the right to call you a terrorist?

40 | What's So Special About Those Killed by Hijackers on September 11, 2001?

As I write, on September 11, 2003, anyone who is listening to the radio, watching television, or reading a newspaper is being reminded that today is the second anniversary of the infamous terrorist attacks. Indeed, the news media have been alerting everybody for weeks that this anniversary was imminent and inviting us to participate, if only as spectators, in some species of choreographed remembrance.

Although I, like all other civilized persons the world over, recoiled at the horror of so many innocent lives taken when the hijackers turned fuel-laden airliners into incendiary missiles and crashed them into skyscrapers crowded with people, I cannot help feeling at this point—indeed, I have been feeling for some time—that the remembrance of these terrible events has become maudlin and subject to more than one sort of self-interested exploitation.

Of course, the mass media have no shame. They will supply anything that they expect will attract consumers to their product, no matter how emotionally spurious it might be. Tearjerkers are part of their stock in trade, and the events of 9/11 can serve as an inexhaustible wellspring of manipulable emotions. Have the relatives of the victims of any other great tragedy received comparable solicitude or such extensive, persistent consideration?

On any given day in the United States, more than six thousand people die. Although some are elderly and may be viewed as persons whose inevitable "time has come," others perish tragically, because they are young or because they are especially worthy and still full of potential. Many persons just leave home for work or shopping and never return, being cut down by accidents or cardiac arrest. Some are murdered—on a typical day about fifty homicides occur. We may presume then that on September 11, 2001, for every person who died at the hands of the murderous hijackers, more than two other persons died in other ways. Why do the deaths of the Twin Towers decedents merit such lavish remembrance, whereas the deaths of others whose lives ended on that day merit no remembrance at all? Is there something memorably heroic about having happened to be in the wrong building at an unfortunate moment?

Perhaps the 9/11 deaths stir such hyperemotional fascination because so many persons perished together. Nobody can know about or keep track of all the thousands of separate deaths that normally occur across the country each day, but everybody can remember just two big adjacent buildings falling down only minutes apart.

Neither the government nor the media, however, make a big ado about commemorating the events of April 19, 1995, when another devastating terrorist attack mangled the Murrah Federal Building in Oklahoma City, killing 167 persons (including 19 children) and injuring another 675 persons who required medical treatment. Might the relative lack of interest in recalling this calamitous attack have something to do with its having been mounted by a native-born American and veteran of the U.S. Army rather than by Arab Muslim zealots? Might the apparent eagerness to forget the attack and its victims spring from the government's desire to discourage the recollection of what motivated it—namely, the government's own murderous assault on the Branch Davidians at Waco precisely two years earlier?

I have a hypothesis about why the government and its lapdog media continue to stimulate such bloated observance of the tragedy of September 11. I maintain that doing so helps greatly to justify the government's initiation and continued prosecution of its current spate of military campaigns, conquests, and occupations in Southwest Asia. Even though the Bush administration has never produced a shred of credible evidence that Saddam Hussein's regime had anything to do with the 9/11 attacks, the administration has never ceased to claim or to insinuate that some "link" existed. This big lie, persistently repeated, has had a big payoff. According to an IBD/TIPP poll conducted during the first week of September 2003, some 63 percent of the respondents believe that al Qaeda and the old Iraqi regime were connected.

The 9/11 attack, then, is to the Bush administration as the Pearl Harbor attack was to the Roosevelt administration: an enduringly evocative pretext for whatever "retaliatory" measures the government chooses to take, even if, as in the present case, the retaliation is aimed in large part at parties who had nothing to do with the initial attack. (A year before the 9/11 attacks the neocon Project for the New American Century, whose members included Dick Cheney, Donald Rumsfeld, and Paul Wolfowitz, seeking to build up the military, noted the need for a "catastrophic and catalyzing event—like a new Pearl Harbor.") Every time that Americans relive the tragedy of September 11, their blood boils, and they yearn to lash out at the responsible parties, or, if not at them, then at somebody who bears a vague resemblance to them.

So we can expect from here on to be bombarded with annual observances that are on the one hand tearfully sentimental and on the other hand implicitly if not explicitly jingoistic. The core message will remain: weep, but don't just sit there crying forever; get up and kill somebody—or better yet, support with great cheer your government as it does the killing in your name.

41

The Crimes at Abu Ghraib Are Not the Worst

Recent days have been hectic for the Supreme Rulers in Washington, D.C. President George W. Bush and Secretary of Defense Donald Rumsfeld have ceased their accustomed swaggering, put on their most somber faces, and issued one apology after another for the mistreatment of prisoners by U.S. soldiers and mercenaries at Abu Ghraib prison. Although the government has known about these disgusting, sadistic, and idiotic amusements for a long time, Rumsfeld kept a close hold on the information, the better to brush it under the official rug. (We know that the government knew because the International Committee for the Red Cross, which made several inspections of the prisons in Iraq, confirms that long ago it "told the Americans that what was going on at Abu Ghraib is reprehensible.") Once the photos got out, of course, more than one kind of hell broke loose, and now the government's top dogs all have their tails tucked shamefully between their legs. South Carolina senator Lindsey Graham warned reporters after Rumsfeld's Senate interrogation on May 7 that "there's more to come," and "we're talking about rape and murder and some very serious charges" against U.S. soldiers and civilian employees in Iraq.

Although Bush says that he is sorry for "the terrible and horrible acts," and Rumsfeld says that he takes "full responsibility," the president continues to express confidence in his defense secretary, and the secretary says that he has no intention of stepping down. Which is to say, neither of these men foresees bearing any real personal cost whatsoever, aside from the momentary embarrassment, the political discomposure, and the time expended in spinning the issue for Congress and the public. Meanwhile, the administration is working overtime to pin the blame on some low-level patsies so that everybody can get on with campaigning for Bush's reelection.

Although no principle stands higher in military doctrine than that the commander bears full responsibility for the actions of his subordinates, neither of these two top military commanders has the decency to resign—not just on account of the prison disclosures, of course, but also on account of the plethora of actions by which they have abused their constitutional powers and brought everlasting shame upon the United States—and nobody is in a position to dismiss them except the spineless Congress, whose members would sooner cut off their arms and legs than impeach Bush for his war crimes.

And make no mistake: plenty of war crimes have been and continue to be committed for which these men, along with many other civilian and military agents of the government, bear full responsibility. After all, in violation of the rule the Allies enforced against the Nazis at the post–World War II Nuremburg Trials, they chose to launch an aggressive, unprovoked, and unnecessary war against the Iraqi people and during the past year have undertaken to impose U.S. domination on the conquered people by rampant military violence. That many Iraqis have fought back against their occupiers in no way justifies U.S. actions. Everyone has a right of self-defense. What would you do if your country had been occupied by murderous and sadistic foreign troops?

The worst U.S. crimes in Iraq have received far less press than the photos of U.S. soldiers having fun and games with the prisoners at Abu Ghraib—not that the prisoners were anything but terrified by these vile amusements—but the truly terrible crimes have not gone totally unreported, especially in the news media outside the United States.

Last May 11 one of the thousands of such stories somehow made its way into the *New York Times*. It told how on April 5, 2003, a home in Basra had been hit by a U.S. bomb that exploded and killed ten members of Abed Hassan Hamoodi's extended family. British military officials said they had received reports that General Ali Hassan al-Majid—the notorious "Chemical Ali"—was in the neighborhood. Of course, the attack, which demolished a number of houses and killed twenty-three of their occupants, failed to kill al-Majid. (In the phrase *military intelligence,* emphasis should always be placed on the word *military.*) But one of the bombs brought an end to most members of Hamoodi's family.

"Ammar Muhammad was not yet 2 when his grandfather pulled him from the rubble and tried to give him mouth-to-mouth resuscitation, but his mouth was full of dust and he died." Seventy-two-year-old Hamoodi declared that he considered the destruction of his home and the killings of his family members to constitute a war crime, and he asked rhetorically: "How would President Bush feel if he had to dig his daughters from out of the rubble?"

How indeed?

U.S. forces have expended thousands of cluster munitions in Iraq, often in heavily populated places. (In the Karbala-Hillah area alone, U.S. teams had destroyed by late August last year more than thirty-one thousand unexploded bomblets "that landed on fields, homes, factories and roads . . . many were in populated areas on Karbala's outskirts.") The toll among children, whose natural curiosity draws them to the interesting-looking bomblets, has been heavy.

Khalid Tamimi and four other members of his family were walking on a footpath in Baghdad when his brother, seven-year-old Haithem, spotted something interesting, picked it up and examined it, then threw it down. The bomblet's explosion killed Haithem and his nine-year-old cousin, Nora, and seriously wounded Khalid, as well as the children's mothers, Amal and Mayasa.

Last year the whole world learned about Ali Ismail Abbas, the twelve-year-old boy who was sleeping in his home in Baghdad when a U.S. missile struck, and the explosion tore off both his arms and killed his parents and his brother. The heartrending photo of him appeared in news media around the world, as did reports of his anguished cries for help in getting his arms back.

Recently, the ferocious U.S. attacks on Fallujah have yielded hundreds of additional casualties among the innocent. There, as in many other places in Iraq, U.S. troops have fired recklessly and without adequate regard for the thousands of civilians they thereby placed in mortal jeopardy. "I'm sitting at the funeral of my only son, who was killed because of the U.S. Marines' harsh manner in dealing with civilians," Abbas Abdullah told a reporter for the *Los Angeles Times.* "They shot him in the head, and he died instantly."

In the White House Rose Garden on April 30, President Bush, displaying his usual keen sensitivity, blustered as he often has on the campaign trail that, because of the U.S. invasion, "there are no longer torture chambers or rape rooms or mass graves in Iraq." The president made this claim even as the whole world's press was featuring photos of the U.S. torture chambers at Abu Ghraib and reporting worse crimes against Iraqi detainees there and elsewhere, including rape and murder.

Moreover, mass graves have been filling up for weeks at Fallujah, for the most part with noncombatants. According to Dahr Jamail's report in *The Nation,* "two soccer fields in Fallujah have been converted to graveyards." Jamail also reported that "the Americans have bombed one hospital, and, numerous sources told us, were sniping at people who attempted to enter and exit the other major medical facility." Snipers also shot ambulances braving the dangerous streets to bring the wounded to makeshift places of medical assistance.

Along a quiet residential street in Fallujah, nine-year-old Rahad Septi and other children were playing hide-and-seek when the pilot of a U.S. A-10 aircraft dropped a bomb there. Rahad, "Little Flower" to her father, Juma Septi, was killed along with ten other children, and twelve other children were wounded. Three adults also were killed. Jamal Abbas was driving his taxi when the bomb fell. He found his eleven-year-old niece Arij Haki with "the top half of her head . . . blown off." After half an hour of searching amid the devastation, Abbas found his daughter, eleven-year-old Miad Jamal Abbas, "her body bloody and ripped." She died later at the hospital. "There was no military activity in this area," said Saad Ibrahim, whose father Hussein was killed in his nearby shop by the same bomb blast. "There was no shooting. This is not a military camp. These are houses with children playing in the street."

When Daham Kassim, his wife, Gufran Ibed Kassim, and their four children tried to escape the hell of U.S. bombing in their neighborhood in Nasiriyah, they stopped on the outskirts of the city at a military checkpoint, where, without warning, U.S. tank crews blasted their car with machine-gun fire, killing three of the children and wounding all the other occupants of the car. U.S. troops, humanitarian as ever, then took the three survivors of the attack to a field hospital, treated their wounds, and let them rest in beds. On the third night, however, the troops expelled them from the hospital to make room for wounded U.S. soldiers. As Kassim relates the story, "They carried us like dogs, out into the cold, without shelter, or a blanket. It was the days of the sandstorms and freezing at night. And I heard [five-year-old] Zainab crying: 'Papa, Papa, I am cold, I am cold.' Then she went silent. Completely silent. . . . My arms were broken. I could not lift or hold her. . . . We had to sit there, and listen to her die."

In Nasiriyah, only Kadem Hashem and his youngest daughter survived when a U.S. missile struck their house. His wife, Salima, five of their children, and six other family members who happened to be in the house at the time were killed. Finding a photograph in the debris of his house, Hashem told reporter Ed Vulliamy of *The Observer:* "This was my middle daughter, Hamadi. I found her burnt to death by that doorway, she had shrunk to about a metre tall." His one surviving daughter, Bedour, described now as "what remains of a beautiful girl," lies on the floor of a relative's house. "She is shrivelled and petrified like a dead cat. Her skin is like scorched parchment folded over her bones. Unable to move, she appears as if in some troubled coma, but opens her eyes, with difficulty, to issue an indecipherable cry like a wounded animal." Hashem dug a mass grave for his family in a nearby holy city. "I collected them all and put them in a single grave at Najaf; my money was burnt, too, and I couldn't afford to bury them separately."

To my knowledge, neither President Bush nor Vice President Dick Cheney nor Secretary of State Colin Powell nor Secretary of Defense Rumsfeld nor Deputy Secretary of Defense Paul Wolfowitz nor Under Secretary of Defense Douglas Feith nor Richard Perle (who has worked for decades at the highest levels both inside and outside the government to bring about the present horrors in Iraq)—not a single one of them has apologized to any of the victims identified in the foregoing accounts.

What the U.S. government did at Abu Ghraib was bad, but what it did to Ammar Muhammad, to Haithem Tamimi, to Ali Ismail Abbas, to Abbas Abdullah's son, to Rahad Septi, to Arij Haki, to Miad Jamal Abbas, to Zainab Kassim, and to Bedour Hashem was far, far worse.

Their stories are but a very few of the tens of thousands that might be told if more complete information were available to provide the details associated with the gruesome statistics on deaths and injuries among the Iraqi population. Relatively few of the people slain were "terrorists," Baathists, or even insurgents. Most were noncombatants; thousands were women, children, and elderly people. The military euphemism for these deaths is "collateral damage," but they are actually murders. After all, they did not happen by accident; in the circumstances, they were as predictable as the sun's rising in the east. By choosing to engage in the kinds of military actions that made these deaths inevitable, the U.S. government thereby chose to cause these deaths. The claim that they were not intended has no substance whatsoever.

Bush and Rumsfeld have been busy with apologies this past week, to be sure, and the prison hijinks at Abu Ghraib certainly cry out for apologies, as well as for a great deal of additional effort to restrain the sadists and sexual psychopaths among the U.S. troops in Iraq and to bring some measure of justice to those who have been wronged. Yet this whole mess, its powerful symbolism notwithstanding, has constituted a gigantic distraction from the truly monstrous crimes committed, and still being committed daily, by U.S. forces in Iraq.

Saddam Hussein now languishes in U.S. custody; his government has been overthrown; no weapons of mass destruction existed in Iraq, and therefore "disarming" the Iraqis of such weapons proved unnecessary. In short, the declared U.S. mission has long since been accomplished fully. Why then does the U.S. government persist in slaughtering the Iraqi people?

42 | Has the U.S. Government Committed War Crimes in Afghanistan and Iraq?

After World War II, the U.S. government, in cooperation with the governments of the United Kingdom, the Soviet Union, and France, established an International Military Tribunal to bring to justice the leaders of the European Axis regimes. The tribunal's charter, published August 8, 1945, declared in Article 6: "The following acts, or any of them, are crimes coming within the jurisdiction of the Tribunal for which there shall be individual responsibility":

(*a*) Crimes against Peace: namely, planning, preparation, initiation or waging of a war of aggression, or a war in violation of international treaties, agreements or assurances, or participation in a Common Plan or Conspiracy for the accomplishment of any of the foregoing;

(*b*) War Crimes: namely, violations of the laws or customs of war. Such violations shall include, but not be limited to, murder, ill-treatment or deportation to slave labor or for any other purpose of civilian population of or in occupied territory, murder or ill-treatment of prisoners of war or persons on the seas, killing of hostages, plunder of public or private property, wanton destruction of cities, towns, or villages, or devastation not justified by military necessity;

(*c*) Crimes against Humanity: namely, murder, extermination, enslavement, deportation, and other inhumane acts committed against any civilian population, before or during the war, or persecutions on political, racial, or religious grounds in execution of or in connection with any crime within the jurisdiction of the Tribunal, whether or not in violation of domestic law of the country where perpetrated.

The article concluded by declaring pointedly that "leaders, organizers, instigators, and accomplices participating in the formulation of execution of a Common Plan or Conspiracy to commit any of the foregoing crimes are responsible for all acts performed by any persons in execution of such plan."

Further, Section 7 states: "The official position of defendants, whether as Heads of State or responsible officials in Government departments, shall not be considered as freeing them from responsibility or mitigating punishment." Moreover, Section 8 states: "The fact that the defendant acted pursuant to order of his Government or of a superior shall not free him from responsibility." The tribunal also prohibited *tu quoque* (so did you) defenses—no surprise, inasmuch as this whole proceeding amounted to "victor's justice," and the prosecuting powers themselves scarcely wished to acknowledge that during the war they too had taken many actions that would not bear scrutiny.

At a series of trials at Nuremberg from 1945 to 1949, more than one hundred defendants were tried. At the most important trial, which placed before the bar of justice the top surviving leaders of Hitler's government, twenty-two men were indicted on one or more of the counts listed above; nineteen were convicted on one or more counts; and three were found not guilty. Of those found guilty, twelve were sentenced to death by hanging; three were sentenced to life in prison; and four were sentenced to prison for terms that varied from ten to twenty years. No appeals were permitted.

If today the U.S. government were to put *itself* on trial, on the same basis it employed to try the Nazis at Nuremberg, for actions taken in Afghanistan and Iraq in recent years, it might have to convict itself—if only for the sake of consistency. Justice is no respecter of person. Can anyone sincerely maintain that what was a crime for Hermann Göring and Alfred Jodl is not equally a crime for Donald Rumsfeld and Dick Cheney?

Evidently, leaders of the Bush administration have given serious consideration to the possibility that their actions might lead to an indictment for war crimes, and they have taken legal measures to minimize their exposure to such prosecution. In a January 25, 2002, memorandum obtained and publicized recently by *Newsweek,* Alberto R. Gonzales, counsel to the president, outlined the pros and cons of the government's decisions about the treatment of prisoners in the so-called war on terrorism. Gonzales agreed with President George W. Bush that because "the war against terrorism is a new kind of war," the Geneva Convention III on the Treatment of Prisoners of War need not be heeded. As Gonzales wrote, "this new paradigm renders obsolete Geneva's strict limitations on questioning of enemy prisoners and renders quaint some of its provisions. . . . [It] eliminates any argument regarding the need for case-by-case determinations of POW status." An official presidential determination that the Geneva Convention "does not apply to al Qaeda and the Taliban," Gonzales opined, "substantially reduces the threat of domestic criminal prosecution under the War Crimes Act (18 U.S.C. 2441)." That statute, he added pointedly, "prohibits the commission of a 'war crime' by or against a U.S. person, including U.S. officials. . . . Adhering to your determination that [the Geneva Convention] does not apply would guard effectively against misconstruction or misapplication of [the War Crimes Act]" and thus would serve as "a solid defense to any future prosecution."

Not for nothing were administration officials worried about a potential indictment for war crimes. I am neither a lawyer nor an expert on the Geneva Conventions, but as I consider how the U.S. government planned its recent military actions in Afghanistan and Iraq and how it has conducted—and continues to conduct—those actions, I encounter time and again prima facie evidence that U.S. leaders and their armed forces in the field have committed crimes against peace, war crimes, and crimes against humanity as defined by the Charter of the International Military Tribunal at Nuremberg in 1945.

First, in the light of voluminous evidence now available to everybody, it seems clear that leaders and advisers of the Bush administration engaged in "planning, preparation, initiation or waging of a war of aggression." After all, Iraq posed no threat to the United States. Its government had neither the means nor the intention of waging war against this country; nor did it issue any threat to harm the United States. That high officials of the U.S. government and their supporters in the news media and elsewhere openly made many false statements to justify the invasion and occupation of Iraq surely exonerates nobody; if anything, those statements cast the guilty parties in an even starker light.

Second, in the light of voluminous evidence now available to everybody, it seems clear that Bush administration leaders and military personnel acting in obedience to those leaders have committed "violations of the laws or customs of war," including "murder . . . of civilian population of or in occupied territory, murder or ill-treatment of prisoners of war . . . plunder of public or private property, wanton destruction of cities, towns, or villages, or devastation not justified by military necessity." The perpetrators' baseless pleas of military necessity, of course, cannot absolve them for their actual crimes as defined above.

The latest outrage, reported in the *Washington Post* on May 20, 2004, involved the killing by U.S. forces of more than forty civilians, most of them women and children, in the village of Makr al-Deeb in western Iraq. A U.S. military official in Baghdad said that "our sense is that this was a legitimate military target. We suspect that this was a smuggler or foreign-fighter [camp]." "It's our estimation right now that the [Iraqi] personnel involved in this matter were part of the foreign-fighter safe house." So, on the basis of *suspicion* of trafficking in unauthorized migrants, U.S. military forces, without warning, used aerial bombardments and strafing with high-powered guns to obliterate an entire village. An Iraqi witness at the scene told the Associated Press Television Network: "The planes came in and shot the whole family. They kept shooting [from approximately 2:45 A.M.] until the morning, until they destroyed all the houses. They didn't leave anything." In a May 21 follow-up report, Associated Press writer Scheherezade Faramarzi quoted a survivor of the attack, Madhi Nawaf, who said: "One of [the dead] was my daughter. I found her a few steps from the house, her 2-year-old son Raad in her arms. Her 1-year-old son, Raed, was lying nearby, missing his head."

U.S. forces claim that they were fired upon first, but Iraqis on the scene maintain that the Americans attacked people who had gathered in the village the previous evening for a wedding celebration and that no shooting had taken place prior to the U.S. attack. Regardless of whether U.S. intelligence about a "foreign-fighter safe house" happened to be accurate or not, however, the killing of the village's noncombatant inhabitants willy-nilly, firing from aircraft at a distance too great to discriminate among persons in targeting and using bombs that cannot discriminate in any event, looks very much like a war crime. Another survivor of the attack, Sheik Dahan Haraj, denied the U.S. claims and asked the obvious question: If the American soldiers suspected that foreign fighters were in the village, "why not seal off the area and make sure they were indeed foreign fighters?"

In any event, the U.S. action was in this case, as it has been in countless others, wholly out of proportion to the underlying justification. This sort of attack has been going on in Afghanistan for almost three years and in Iraq ever since the U.S. invasion began in March 2003. Anybody can easily fill a cabinet with such news reports filed by journalists from many different countries. As Human Rights Watch concluded in a report last October, U.S. actions "reveal a pattern of over-aggressive tactics, excessive shooting in residential areas and hasty reliance on lethal force."

Although the U.S. commanders exhibit insouciance about civilian casualties among the Afghan and Iraqi populations—in the immortal words of General Tommy Franks, "We don't do body counts"—responsible estimates of the number of civilians killed in the recent U.S. military actions range from one thousand to five thousand in Afghanistan and from nine thousand to eleven thousand (in some estimates as many as thirty-five thousand or more) in Iraq. In addition, thousands of noncombatants have been wounded seriously or have suffered the wanton destruction of their homes and other property. Still, every day the grisly toll continues to mount.

Thus, "crimes against humanity," including "murder . . . and other inhumane acts committed against any civilian population," seem sufficiently obvious to justify a prosecution under the terms of the Nuremberg Tribunal.

Anyone can guess, of course, how the perpetrators of these crimes might seek to excuse their actions—worse yet, to take public credit for them and to seek reelection to public office on the basis of having taken them proudly and enthusiastically, while swathed magnificently in the *Stars and Stripes* (exception being made for the now globally publicized "abuse" of prisoners, of course, those actions having been officially designated as "un-American"). But just recall how far the Nazis got at Nuremberg when they invoked the same sorts of excuses. Did not Göring plead, for example, that operation of the concentration camps was necessary to preserve order? Did he not say, "It was a question of removing danger"?

No surprise, of course, if accused criminals offer excuses for their crimes—although Hitler's minister of munitions Albert Speer was remarkably contrite at Nuremberg, saying, "it is my unquestionable duty to assume my share of responsibility for the disaster of the German people." Especially rare is admission of guilt by government officials: rulers and state functionaries habitually consider themselves above the laws that apply to other people. In Shakespeare's *Richard III*, even bloodstained Gloucester had an excuse, but Lady Anne, the slain king's widow, amidst the aftermath of the mayhem, was not buying it: "Fouler than heart can think thee, thou canst make no excuse, but to hang thyself." As Lady Anne said to Gloucester, so others now might say to the leaders of the U.S. government:

> For thou hast made the happy earth thy hell,
> Fill'd it with cursing cries and deep exclaims.
> If thou delight to view thy heinous deeds,
> Behold this pattern of thy butcheries.

We need not prejudge, of course. Let all the accused have their day in court. Consistency requires nothing less.

PART VIII

Cake Walk

43

WMD Blues

Well I woke up dis mo'nin'
My head had a screw lo'se
Went down to de co'nah
Gonna find out de late news
But I jist couldn't shake'm
Dem WMD blues.
I got de W
I got de W
I got de W
MD blues.

Well de man on de TV
Say de president's sho
Dat de 'raqis dey gonna
Cough up where dey are
But I jist cain't shake'm
Dem WMD blues.
I got de W
I got de W
I got de W
MD blues.

Dem boys ove'n Baghdad
Dey be having a fit
'cause no matter who dey grab
Dey ain't findin' shit.
Fo' too long dey sho gonna git

Originally appeared August 15, 2003

Dem WMD blues.
Dey'll git de W
Dey'll git de W
Dey'll git de W
MD blues.

Ol' Rumsfel' be huffing
He be lookin' in holes
He be shoutin' 'n' puffin'
He be lookin' up poles.
Still he ain't got nuthin'
But de WMD blues.
He got de W
He got de W
He got de W
MD blues.

Well Wolfie be howlin'
And he be a growlin'
He done made it known
'less'n we plant dat shit
Den he sho gonna git
Dem WMD blues.
He'll have de W
He'll have de W
He'll have de W
MD blues (sho nuf).

My woman done lef' me
My boss fired my ass
My wadah been shut off
My car it won't start
But for sho de wust part be
Dem WMD blues

I got de W
I got de W
I got de W
MD blues (fo' sho).

(Dat's all.)

Lyrics transcribed from a live performance by the venerable blues-man Buck "One Horse" Higgs at the Fourteenth Avenue House of Blues in Covington, Louisiana.

44

Taking Stock One Year after the U.S. Invasion of Iraq

One year ago the United States unleashed its armed forces in an invasion of Iraq. Prior to the invasion, the Bush administration offered a variety of justifications for launching it and defended its war plan against critics who claimed that a U.S. invasion was unnecessary and would be immoral or unwise. For everyone except those blinded by partisan loyalty to the Bush administration, the truth is now all too obvious. The administration was wrong, and the critics were right.

The president, the vice president, the secretaries of defense and state, and other leading figures in the Bush administration insisted confidently and repeatedly in interviews, speeches, and public forums that the Iraqi regime harbored vast stocks of chemical and biological weapons; that it was actively developing nuclear weapons; that it either possessed already or soon would possess effective means, including long-range missiles and unmanned aerial vehicles, of delivering so-called weapons of mass destruction far beyond its borders, even to the United States; that it had established links to members of al Qaeda; and that it was directing its military and related efforts toward wreaking great harm on the United States. Along the way, many auxiliary claims came forth involving, among other things, an alleged Iraqi attempt to obtain uranium "yellow cake" from Niger; procurement of aluminum tubes allegedly for use in Iraqi nuclear-weapons production; and an alleged April 2001 meeting in Prague between al Qaeda operative Mohammed Atta and an Iraqi intelligence agent. Administration leaders maintained that the conquest of Iraq (officially its "liberation") would set off a chain reaction of democratization across the Middle East.

Originally appeared March 18, 2004

On March 17, 2003, just two days before the beginning of the U.S. invasion, President Bush said in an evening address to the nation:

> Intelligence gathered by this and other governments leaves no doubt that the Iraq regime continues to possess and conceal some of the most lethal weapons ever devised. . . . The [Iraqi] regime . . . has aided, trained and harbored terrorists, including operatives of al Qaeda. The danger is clear: Using chemical, biological or, one day, nuclear weapons obtained with the help of Iraq, the terrorists could fulfill their stated ambitions and kill thousands or hundreds of thousands of innocent people in our country or any other. . . . Before the day of horror can come, before it is too late to act, this danger will be removed. . . . The tyrant will soon be gone. [Iraqi people,] [t]he day of your liberation is near. . . . [W]e cannot live under the threat of blackmail. The terrorist threat to America and the world will be diminished the moment that Saddam Hussein is disarmed. . . . We are now acting because the risks of inaction would be far greater. . . . We choose to meet that threat now where it arises, before it can appear suddenly in our skies and cities. . . . [R]esponding to such enemies only after they have struck first is not self-defense. It is suicide. The security of the world requires disarming Saddam Hussein now. . . . [W]hen the dictator has departed, [the Iraqi people] can set an example to all the Middle East of a vital and peaceful and self-governing nation.

On March 19, having ordered U.S. forces to begin the invasion, the president said in an evening address:

> We have no ambition in Iraq, except to remove a threat and restore control of that country to its own people. . . . Our nation enters this conflict reluctantly, yet our purpose is sure. The people of the United States and our friends and allies will not live at the mercy of an outlaw regime that threatens the peace with weapons of mass murder. . . . We will meet that threat now with our Army, Air Force, Navy, Coast Guard and Marines, so that we do not have to meet it later with armies of firefighters and police and doctors on the streets of our cities.

Despite a lingering unwillingness to admit in plain language that none of the president's claims about Iraqi threats has held up in the face of the facts brought to light during the past year, the administration has ceased to defend these claims and has resorted instead to denying that the president himself ever used the phrase *imminent threat;* to blaming faulty intelligence for misleading the president; and to justifying the war on the grounds that no matter what else might have been the case, Saddam Hussein was a brutal dictator. Moreover, although the U.S. occupation of Iraq has made that country a magnet for Islamic holy warriors, suicide bombers, and planters of roadside improvised explosive devices (IEDs), and although terrorists have carried out horrendous retaliatory bombings in Saudi Arabia, Morocco, Indonesia, Turkey, and Spain, among other places, President Bush persists in his locker-room bravado and declares that the U.S. invasion and occupation of Iraq have made the world "a safer, freer place."

Today, many prewar predictions can be tested against the actual outcomes of the war. We now know, for example, that U.S. forces have not been welcomed—at least, not for long or by many people—in Iraq. But in view of the thousands of deaths that they caused among civilians as well as among Iraqi soldiers, the countless persons of all ages and both sexes that they injured, the vast destruction of property that they wreaked, and the widespread looting that they unleashed and then stood by watching, why would they have been welcomed? Many Iraqis, especially the Shiites and Kurds, are pleased to be rid of Saddam Hussein and his regime, but few of them relish the occupation of their country by U.S. troops or their subjugation to a foreign power. In the port city of Umm Qasr, hospital director Dr. Akram Gataa gave representative testimony for the southern region when he said, "Everyone was happy when the soldiers came here to get rid of the old regime, but now people are wondering what this so-called freedom has brought them." Dr. Gataa reported that the mood of the local people was turning quickly from frustration to resentment and anger, and he added: "All of us will fight them if they stay here too long. No Iraqi will accept this turning into the occupation of their country."

Nor do the U.S. troops themselves enjoy serving as targets in the scores of attempts made daily to kill them. As one soldier said, "U.S. officials need to get our asses out of here. We have no business being here. . . . All we are here is potential people to be killed and sitting ducks." Nearly six hundred have died so far, thousands have been injured seriously, and many have had their mental states rearranged for the worse—approximately one thousand of the U.S. troops evacuated to Landstuhl Regional Medical Center in Germany were suffering from mental problems, according to hospital commander Colonel Rhonda Cornum. Violence can accomplish certain things, but neither "nation building" nor the promotion of sound mental health is among those things.

For many of us, none of these events has come as a surprise. Before the war, we told anyone who would listen that the administration had not made a convincing case for its impending invasion of Iraq and that its rosy forecast of the aftermath of a U.S. attack was so unlikely as to border on the fantastical.

Because the prosecution of a war serves so splendidly to promote government power and to gratify a president's delusions of war-leader "greatness" (his prime claim to fame as he seeks reelection), however, one naturally suspects that the invasion of Iraq was never intended to serve the announced purposes, that the stated rationale was pure pretext all along. A close look at the backgrounds, expressed policy preferences, and actions of the neoconservative schemers who played such a prominent role in promoting the invasion—Dick Cheney, Donald Rumsfeld, Richard Perle, Paul Wolfowitz, Douglas Feith, and company—does nothing to diminish such suspicion. Indeed, if the pure-pretext explanation is not valid, then one is hard pressed to understand how the government, with its vast multi-billion-dollar intelligence apparatus, managed to get so many things wrong while isolated individuals with no privileged access to classified or inside information, such as I, managed to get them right all along.

Truth be known, this discrepancy testifies to the comic-opera quality of the whole undertaking. It illuminates the many ways in which the administration, the so-called intelligence community, the make-believe checks and balances in Congress and the courts, and the propaganda organs that masquerade as major independent news media have been engaged and even now continue to engage in something akin to one of those huge ballroom dances at the Palace of Versailles, each dancer moving in perfect harmony with all the rest, almost as if the entire performance had been—dare I say?—choreographed. Gazing though the unshuttered windows of power at this grandiose performance, the awed peasants perceive the elegantly costumed and magnificently coiffured dancers as they join and turn and separate, only to join and turn again in harmonious synchronization.

Thus, the Democratic challenger for the presidency is represented by his party and by the press as a stern critic of the war, but one has to wonder: Where was his steely resolve in October 2002, when he voted in the Senate to hand over to the president the authority that the Constitution gives to Congress alone to declare war? Now, weaseling like a typical politician, he maintains that he was tricked—Bush "misled every one of us," he declares—and that he voted as he did because he trusted George Bush to go to war only as a "last resort." Can John Kerry have been so obtuse that he had no idea who held the reins at the Bush administration? Did he not know what Cheney, Rumsfeld, Wolfowitz, Feith, and the rest of that gang had been cooking up for decades in public as well as in private? Clarifying his stance, Kerry maintains not that Bush should not have gone to war, but only that Bush should have formed a bigger coalition before doing so. Evidently an immoral and unwise war is hunky-dory if enough aggressors join forces to wage it.

To suppose that Kerry is antiwar and Bush pro-war would be to mischaracterize a case of Tweedle Dumb and Tweedle Dumber. As a phrase used on another, similar occasion back in the 1960s reminds us, there's not a dime's worth of difference between these two barons of the ruling oligarchy. The effusion of campaign blather and the election that will mercifully end it in November are all part of the ritual dance. In no event will the election's outcome materially affect the realities of death and destruction that U.S. and puppet forces are dishing out worldwide or the spasms of terrorist retaliation and assorted other "blowback" that are certain to follow. To imagine anything else is tantamount to forgetting the entire political history of this country during the past century.

Meanwhile, the dance continues. A congressionally approved blue-ribbon commission, though repeatedly obstructed by the president's refusal to cooperate fully, strenuously probes the 9/11 disaster in preparation for its eventual preordained whitewash of presidential or administration responsibility. Another bipartisan, presidentially appointed panel, whose report has been conveniently scheduled to arrive well after the November election, digs into the "faulty intelligence" on which the administration relied prior to its invasion of Iraq. Weapons searcher David Kay has already admitted that "we were almost all wrong," and the commission's goal of course is to "get to the bottom" of this matter—as if, at this late date, the whole world doesn't know exactly how the neocons spun the whole shebang in order to tell a plausible tale on behalf of their beloved war. On Capitol Hill, congressional committees hold mock-serious hearings, going through the motions of searching for the facts about intelligence failures, military snafus, and cozy deals in the military-industrial complex. These dedicated public servants are always shocked—shocked!—when they happen to stumble onto the truth, but as well-rehearsed dancers they can be counted on not to stumble that way frequently. If John Q. Public thinks that any of this official investigatory activity will provide him with reliable information about how the government actually works or even about how it intends to work, he is sacrificing a good opportunity to go fishing. It's all for show.

If you think I'm off base, then take the following test. Check the cast of characters a year from now, five years from now, ten years from now. See who's prospered and who hasn't. See whose head has rolled (don't expect many) for misfeasance or malfeasance in public office. Check whether many politicians who came into office without great wealth somehow left office filthy rich. Check on their friends and relatives, too. Notice whose kids have been killed or wounded by roadside IEDs in whatever Third World hellhole the United States has invaded and occupied most recently (don't expect to find the scions of any government bigwigs among those blown to smithereens or driven mad by combat stress). Check whether the United States has managed to bring into being a glorious worldwide regime of democracy, peace, and prosperity, and whether the world's peoples are hailing Uncle Sam with hosannas and strewing his global pathways with flowers in gratitude for his beneficent intervention (just don't hold your breath waiting for this oft-promised outcome). I'm prepared to be wrong. If I am, I'll deliver a dollar for each of your donuts.

What we see in Iraq one year after the invasion might have been foreseen, and in fact was foreseen, by anybody who cared to take the trouble to look into the matter without ideological or religious blinders and with a modicum of historical background on the conduct of U.S. foreign policy during the past century. This war, like all the others, has been not so much a case of who knew what when, of well-intentioned mistakes and tragic miscalculations. It has been more a case of who told what lies to whom to serve what personal, political, and ideological ends; of who paid the price in blood and treasure, and who came out smelling like a rose; of mendacity and irresponsibility in high places; and of colossal public gullibility in the face of relentless political opportunism. As the saying goes, the more things change . . . .

45

Can Bullets and Bombs Establish Justice in Iraq?

President George W. Bush has said on many occasions that he seeks to "bring to justice" those responsible for the 9/11 attacks on the United States. On September 20, 2001, he told a joint session of Congress: "Whether we bring our enemies to justice or bring justice to our enemies, justice will be done." Later, he associated the U.S. invasion of Iraq with that same quest for justice. Today, however, as violent resistance to the U.S. occupation increases throughout Iraq and as the Shiites as well as the Sunnis fight pitched battles with the occupation forces, the Bush administration's devotion to justice stands clearly revealed as declaration without substance.

Although convincing evidence of alleged cooperation between the Iraqi government and the perpetrators of the 9/11 attacks was never adduced, nobody doubts that Saddam Hussein's regime reeked of injustice, and so the U.S. overthrow of that regime might appear to have been at least consistent with the establishment of justice. The trouble that arose at the very outset, however, reflected the choice of military means to attain the desired end. Notwithstanding all the claims made on behalf of precision weapons, modern warfare always spills over from the guilty to the innocent. Certainly it did so in Iraq, where tens of thousands of men, including many noncombatants, as well as thousands of women and children suffered death or injury as a result of U.S. military actions. Thus were new injustices committed in the process of overthrowing those responsible for old injustices. A net gain for justice?

For U.S. authorities, the question never seemed to arise. On the rare occasions when they recognized that their invasion had entailed any evils at all, they always insisted that those evils amounted to only a small cost relative to the great benefits to be enjoyed by the liberated Iraqi people once the immediate turmoil of the fighting had ceased. All along, however, it was plain that many Iraqis held a different view. Indeed, many were so opposed to the U.S. presence in their country that they tossed not the ballyhooed welcoming flowers, but rocket-propelled grenades and mortar shells at their self-anointed liberators. Saddam Hussein's regime was quickly dispatched, thereby accomplishing the declared U.S. goal, yet the U.S. forces then settled down for an indefinite stay, and many Iraqis continued to fight them tooth and nail at great risk to themselves and their places of residence. What had become of justice?

Listening to U.S. proconsul L. Paul Bremer tell the story, we might never suspect that anything deserves notice in Iraq besides the sweetness and light of the American "reconstruction" of the country's shattered infrastructure and undemocratic institutions. Responding to questions about the recent widespread violence, Bremer declared: "I know if you just report on those few places, it does look chaotic. But if you travel around the country . . . what you find is a bustling economy, people opening businesses right and left, unemployment has dropped." Maybe so, just as after September 11, 2001, almost everything in the United States (except the airlines) continued to operate much as it had before—a few buildings knocked down here and there and four airliners lost out of a fleet of thousands didn't amount, so to speak, to a hill of beans. One suspects, however, that Bremer and other leaders of the Bush administration would vehemently reject this analogous way of putting things into perspective. After all, they have steadfastly insisted that the events of 9/11 "changed everything."

Speaking of the Shiite cleric Muqtada al-Sadr, whose followers have recently joined the fray in several cities, Bremer described the preacher as "a guy who has a fundamentally inappropriate view of the new Iraq." This statement demands close examination. Here is the resident chief of a conquering power seemingly speaking as though he were entitled to say what is appropriate for Iraq. What has happened to government by the consent of the governed? Clearly, although al-Sadr may have little authority to speak for the Iraqi people, Bremer has none at all. Al-Sadr, declared Bremer, "believes that in the new Iraq, like in the old Iraq, power should be to the guy with guns. That is an unacceptable vision for Iraq." It required a great deal of chutzpah for Bremer, who presides over Iraq solely by virtue of the massive firepower of U.S. forces there, to call into question the validity of power that flows from the barrel of a gun. Bremer has utterly no legitimacy as the kingpin of Iraq, and it would be far more becoming if he confined his declarations to topics such as repairs to the water and sewer systems.

In an April 7 press briefing, Defense Secretary Donald H. Rumsfeld described the Iraqi resistance fighters as a few "thugs, gangs, and terrorists." Minimizing the scope of the resistance, he characterized it as consisting of "a small number of terrorists and militias coupled with some protests." (Rumsfeld routinely speaks of all Iraqis who oppose the U.S. occupation as terrorists.) Moreover, in the briefing, he and General Richard Meyers, chairman of the Joint Chiefs of Staff, referred repeatedly to al-Sadr as a murderer. Yet no legitimate court has convicted al-Sadr of murder. To be sure, a certain Iraqi court is said to have indicted him. What should we make of such an indictment? Who composes that court, and how did those persons gain their positions? Clearly, the court has no power to enforce any decision except with the approval and cooperation of U.S. occupation forces. One might have thought that the world had seen enough kangaroo courts during the days of Stalin and Hitler to have acquired some suspicion of judicial integrity in extraordinary circumstances. Yet U.S. authorities display no appreciation of what genuine justice requires for either its determination or its enforcement. There is absolutely no rule of law in Iraq; U.S. forces simply do as they please.

Further evidence of this disregard for justice comes from an anonymous source that the *Wall Street Journal* describes as a "senior Pentagon official." Speaking of previous U.S. deliberations about how to deal with al-Sadr, this official stated, "We've always been really conflicted on how to deal with Sadr. Do you capture or kill him and make him a martyr, or do you ignore him and hope that the Shiites move away from him?" Well, if one seeks to establish justice, one treats him as the rules of justice require. If he is reasonably suspected of having committed a crime, he should be arrested and given a fair trial. In no event, however, is someone who dislikes his sermons or his political views entitled to kill him peremptorily—evidently a live option in discussions among U.S. leaders, according to this nameless official. What sort of justice is it simply to kill an unpopular preacher? Indeed, such a killing would itself seem to be an act of murder that cries out for its perpetrators to be brought to justice.

Meanwhile, here in the tranquil confines of the United States, the dogs of war continue to howl in the mainstream media, and, like the U.S. authorities in Iraq and Washington, D.C., they are howling for further bloodshed, not for justice. (As U.S. Army Lieutenant Colonel Ray Millen recently explained: "'Hearts and minds' is not applicable during a military campaign; that's a long-term solution.") Thus, the *Wall Street Journal*'s editors opined on April 6 that "what's needed now is a reassertion of U.S. resolve. . . . Having let Mr. Sadr's militia grow, the coalition now has no choice but to break it up." Moreover, not content with prescribing bigger doses of U.S. violence in Iraq, the *Journal*'s editors used the occasion to shake their fists at Iran, too. "Iran's mullahs fear a Muslim democracy in Iraq," they asserted, "because it is a direct threat to their own rule. If warnings to Tehran from Washington don't impress them, perhaps some cruise missiles aimed at the Bushehr nuclear site will concentrate their minds."

No one can deny, of course, that incoming cruise missiles do concentrate the mind—the airliners commandeered and turned into guided missiles on 9/11 certainly had that effect on leaders of the Bush administration. Cruise missiles, however, like the five-hundred-pound bombs and M1-A1 tanks being employed to police Iraq today, are not effective instruments for the establishment of justice. There was no justice in the 9/11 attacks on New York City and precious little in the U.S. invasion and occupation of Iraq; nor is any in prospect should the Bush administration loose its firepower gratuitously on Iran. Such employment of indiscriminate force and violence can accomplish certain things—widespread death and destruction above all—but by its very nature it cannot establish justice. Indeed, its most visible effect is the encouragement of recurrent rounds of attack and counterattack. Does anyone really believe that the recent attacks in an arc that stretches from Bali to Istanbul to Madrid were anything but retaliation against people whose governments had cooperated with U.S. military actions in the Middle East? Until the leaders of the U.S. government come to recognize the distinction between waging war and establishing justice, the world will remain at risk of much unnecessary pain and grief.

46

Bush's Iraq War
An Offer You Would Have Refused

Would you have bought into the Iraq War if George W. Bush had made you an honest offer? This question is a revealing variant of one that people often ask and answer: "Is the war worth its price?"

Politicians and government officials are no strangers to such questions, and over the years they have given some amazing—frankly, shocking—answers. Thus, when General Curtis LeMay responded to questions about the U.S. firebombing of Tokyo's residential neighborhoods in the latter stages of World War II, he declared: "We knew we were going to kill a lot of women and kids when we burned that town. Had to be done." That is, the price was acceptable to him.

In 1996, CBS reporter Lesley Stahl, inquiring about the U.S.-led economic sanctions against Iraq, said to UN Ambassador Madeleine Albright: "We have heard that a half million children have died. I mean, that's more children than died in Hiroshima. And—and you know—is the price worth it?" Albright replied: "I think this is a very hard choice, but the price—we think the price is worth it."

Since the Bush administration launched its invasion of Iraq in March 2003, polling organizations have been asking the public from time to time whether they regard this war as worth the price. At first, as always, a large majority replied that it was, but with the passage of time, the mounting of U.S. casualties, and the unhappy course of events on the ground during the protracted U.S. occupation of Iraq, more Americans have come to regard the war's price as too high. In October 2003, after a *CBS News/New York Times* poll had found that "53 percent believe the war was not worth the cost, while just 41 percent believe it was," the president dismissed the poll findings, declaring "I don't make decisions based upon polls. I make decisions based upon what I think is important to the security of the American people."

When the president appeared as Tim Russert's guest on NBC's *Meet the Press* on February 8, 2004, Russert asked, "Is it worth the loss of 530 American lives and 3,000 injuries and woundings simply to remove Saddam Hussein, even though there were no weapons of mass destruction?" Although the president evaded the question and replied with a series of stump-speech declarations and blatantly false claims, he strove to leave the impression that, yes, the price is worth paying.

The costs have continued to mount. Billions of dollars flow steadily from the taxpayers to the Treasury to the military and civilian providers of war goods and services—the current rate of expenditure for specifically Iraq-related military and occupation purposes is approximately $5 billion per month. Two previous emergency appropriations for the Iraq War have provided $149 billion and a recent supplement added $25 billion, but this $174 billion total surely fails to include some war costs included in the regular budget of the Department of Defense. Estimates for the occupation of Iraq in 2005 alone run as high as $75 billion, and the actual expenditures may well turn out to be even greater—government cost overruns are not unheard of, especially in the military-industrial complex. If the true costs of the war to date amount to, say, $200 billion, then the cost is equivalent to approximately $1,850 per household, say, $2,000 in round numbers (if it's not there yet, it will be soon).

Costs in terms of lost life and limb also continue to mount daily. To date, the military authorities have acknowledged more than a thousand deaths and some seven thousand persons seriously wounded or injured among the U.S. forces (according to some unofficial estimates, as many as twelve thousand have been wounded or injured). Many soldiers have been blinded or have lost limbs or have suffered severe psychological traumas from which they will never recover.

Still, the president and his spokesmen, defenders, and supporters stoutly insist that the price is worth paying. The basic problem is that when the question is posed in the usual way, the answers are meaningless.

Consider your situation when you visit an automobile showroom to shop for a new car. The salesman informs you that the model you fancy carries a price tag of, say, $25,000. In considering whether this is a "price worth paying," you do not conduct a public-opinion survey. You do not ask your neighbor or your brother-in-law. You would never think of calling Karl Rove to find out. Only you can answer the question meaningfully, because only you will enjoy the services of the vehicle and only you will bear the sacrifices entailed by your decision to purchase it.

Decisions that government officials make about how to spend your money, whether on the conduct of war or on any other similar governmental undertaking, have a completely different character. In these cases, the government provides a so-called public good, which is to say, a state of affairs that, for better or worse, is the same for everybody. Economists used to argue that owing to the "free-rider problem," only government can provide such public goods, and hence political processes must be employed to decide which projects to undertake and how much of the public's money to spend on each of them.

More recently, however, economists have come to understand that public-good situations can be dealt with more rationally by the use of an arrangement known as a *contingent contract*. This is an agreement in which each member of a group—in this case, each citizen of the United States—is invited to make a certain contribution toward the provision of the resources required to carry out a fully-described all-or-nothing project on the condition that no one must bear his pro rata share of the costs unless a sufficient number of other members accept the same obligation (51 percent, 75 percent, 100 percent of the group's members—whatever is deemed necessary to ensure completion of the project while preserving equity among its expected beneficiaries).

In the case of the Iraq War, for example, the U.S. government, refraining from false advertising, might have presented to each adult living in the United States early in 2003 the following offer. We will bring about a certain state of affairs in Iraq as of September 2004: Saddam Hussein imprisoned and his government overthrown; widespread fighting between U.S troops and resistance forces; extensive public disorder, rampant crime, and personal insecurity; autocratic government and lack of civil liberties; widespread lack of basic public services, such as reliable water supply, sewerage, and electricity supply; and seething political discord among tribal, ethnic, and religious factions struggling to control the country after they have driven out the U.S. occupation forces and their allies. That's what you'll get for your contribution.

In exchange, you and everyone else in the country, should you all agree to the contract, will each make a pro rata financial contribution of $2,000 for each household. In addition, you will each agree to bear your pro rata share of the casualties by participating in a lottery in which each ticket holder will place members of his household at risk of death, injuries, or wounds. Your chance that a household member will be killed is approximately 1 in 108,000, and your chance that a household member will be seriously wounded or injured is approximately 1 in 15,000.

How many citizens do you suppose would have been willing to accept this contract? My guess is almost none. Even if I'm far from guessing correctly, however, I find it inconceivable that enough citizens even to approach forming a majority would have entered voluntarily into this contract. After all, it is an extraordinarily bad deal. In exchange for $2,000 from your personal bank account and a nontrivial chance of death or injury among members of your household, it offers you, well, scarcely anything of value. Even the good part of the deal, the overthrow of the tyrant Saddam Hussein, is unlikely to be worth so much to you; even if you are that rare American who cares deeply about the well-being of the Iraqi people, it's not as if once the old tyrant has been driven from power, everything will be sweetness and light in Iraq—remember, you have been offered an honest deal with an accurate forecast of exactly what the U.S. government will bring about, not a political swindle promising Middle Eastern pie in the sky.

Of course, no politician is about to use contingent contracting to find out what the citizens really want and how urgently they want it. Our rulers already know everything they need to know. They have calculated their own expected political gains and losses, and they have taken into account the gains and losses that will be reaped—often in cold cash—by the coalition of special-interest groups that supports them in holding onto power. The rest of us can resign ourselves to bearing the full costs to our bank accounts as well as to our lives, limbs, and liberties, while our rulers feed us noble-sounding lies and promise us an outcome so lovely and implausible that only God could bring it to pass.

47

The Iraq War—A Catastrophic Success

For where your treasure is, there will your heart be also.

—Matthew 6:21

On the campaign trail last October, Vice President Dick Cheney created a small stir when, speaking of the Iraq war, he declared: "I think it has been a remarkable success story to date when you look at what has been accomplished overall." In view of the rampant violence raging in Iraq, the widespread devastation of the country's human and material resources, and the dim prospects for its future peace and prosperity, Cheney's statement seemed bizarre, and the Democrats seized on it as still another example of the disconnect between the Bush administration and reality. Yet, on closer inspection, we can see that the war has indeed been a huge success, though not exactly in the way that the vice president intended to claim.

In a characteristically unwitting way, President George W. Bush himself stumbled upon a resolution of the seeming paradox when he told *Time* magazine's interviewer last summer that the war had proved to be a "catastrophic success." By that oxymoron, he sought to convey the idea that in the invasion the U.S. military forces had overcome the enemy unexpectedly quickly, "being so successful, so fast, that an enemy that should have surrendered or been done in, escaped and lived to fight another day." Although this hypothesis seems far-fetched as an explanation of the nature and extent of the resistance now being waged against the U.S. occupation forces and their collaborators in Iraq, the term *catastrophic success* does express the character of the war precisely. We need only bear in mind that the catastrophe afflicts one set of people, whereas the success accrues to an entirely different set.

Originally appeared December 21, 2004

Moreover, to appreciate the war's success, we must keep in the forefront of our thinking the instrumental rationality of its perpetrators. We must ask: Who bears the responsibility for launching and continuing the war? What are these individuals trying to achieve? And have they in fact achieved these objectives? Having answered these questions correctly, we shall be obliged to conclude that the war has been a huge success for those who brought it about, however disastrous it has been for many others, especially for the unfortunate people of Iraq.

A short list of the war's perpetrators must include the president and his close advisers; the neoconservative intriguers who stirred up and continue to stoke elite and popular opinion in support of the war; the members of Congress who abdicated their exclusive constitutional responsibility to declare war, authorized the president to take the nation to war if he pleased, and then financed the war by a series of enormous appropriations from the Treasury; and certain politically well-placed persons in the munitions industries and in interest groups that have chosen to support, sometimes for reasons based on religious beliefs, a war that they perceive as promoting Israel's interests or as bringing about the fulfillment of biblical prophecy. Each of these responsible parties has gained greatly from the war.

President Bush sought above all to be reelected. In his 2004 campaign, he made no apologies for the war; indeed, he sought to take credit for launching it and for waging it relentlessly since the invasion. Vice President Cheney also campaigned actively on the same basis. Bush and Cheney's efforts have now yielded them the prize they sought.

In reshuffling his cabinet for a second term, the president has retained the belligerent Donald Rumsfeld as secretary of defense. Paul Wolfowitz, Douglas Feith, and other key warmongers remain in their top positions at the Pentagon, while other neocon desk warriors, such as Lewis "Scooter" Libby, Cheney's chief of staff, and Elliott Abrams, special assistant to the president at the National Security Council, retain their important offices elsewhere in the government—continued success for one and all. Even George "Slam Dunk" Tenet—who resigned as Director of Central Intelligence of his own accord, not because the president held him accountable for the manifest failures of U.S. intelligence efforts during his tenure— recently reemerged to accept the Presidential Medal of Freedom in recognition of what the president described as Tenet's "tireless efforts" in service to the nation. God help us if the next intelligence chief's tireless efforts bring forth equally fatal results.

Members of Congress have no regrets about authorizing Bush to attack Iraq or about continuing to fund the war lavishly. These career politicians crave nothing more than they crave reelection to office, and nearly all the incumbents who sought reelection in the 2004 elections gained this supreme objective: all but one (Tom Daschle) of the 26 incumbent senators running and all but six of the 402 incumbent representatives running succeeded—outcomes that imply a reelection rate greater than 98 percent for incumbents running in both houses combined. Backing the war has obviously proved to be entirely compatible with, if not absolutely essential to, the legislators' quest for continued tenure in office. If as a consequence of these political actions thousands of Iraqi children had to lose their eyesight or their legs or even their lives, well, *c'est la guerre*. Politics is no place for sissies.

While authorizing enormous increases in military spending during the past four years, members of Congress have helped themselves to generous servings of pork from the defense-appropriations bills they have passed. According to Winslow T. Wheeler of the Center for Defense Information in Washington, D.C., "by the time Congress had finished with the bill [fiscal year 2005 appropriations for the Department of Defense] in July [2004], House and Senate members had added more than 2,000 of these 'earmarks'" for home-district projects, thereby dishing out to themselves "a record-setting $8.9 billion in pork" to use in buying votes from their constituents. In this workaday plundering of the taxpayers for wholly self-serving reasons, congressional doves as well as hawks, Democrats as well as Republicans, relish the opportunity to act as pork hawks.

Between fiscal years 2001 and 2004, national-defense outlays, defined narrowly as in the government's official reports, rose by nearly 50 percent (approximately 40 percent after adjustment for inflation). This still-continuing upsurge ranks with the great military buildups of the 1960s and the 1980s. The beauty of all this increased spending, of course, is that every dollar of it lands in somebody's pocket. Those to whom the pockets belong make a practice of lobbying hard for increased military spending, and they are prepared to compensate in various ways, some legal and some not, the politicians and bureaucrats who steer the money in their direction.

Procurement of goods and services from private contractors has been a major item in the increased military spending of recent years. In fiscal year 2000, the top ten contractors together received prime contract awards of $50.6 billion; just three years later, in fiscal year 2003, they got $82.7 billion—an increase of 63 percent (well in excess of 50 percent even after a generous adjustment for inflation).

Lockheed Martin, Boeing, Northrop Grumman, General Dynamics, and Raytheon are the biggest boys on this block nowadays, but lest anyone think that an aspiring smaller fellow cannot play in this league, let Halliburton serve as an inspiring counterexample. Back in fiscal year 2001, this company ranked thirty-seventh among the Defense department's prime contractors. Thanks to the war and Halliburton's foot in the door as oil-field-service expert and caterer to the troops in Iraq and its environs, the company leaped to seventh place in the rankings in fiscal year 2003, with prime contracts in that year valued at $3.9 billion. Furthermore, even this outstanding corporate success seems to have been but a springboard to greater accomplishments. By the end of 2004, Halliburton's contracts for Iraq work had accumulated to approximately $10.8 billion, with more in the works.

Notwithstanding the success that Halliburton, Bechtel, Dyncorp, and other "old boy" service contractors have achieved in connection with the Iraq war, the really big military money still goes to the suppliers of whiz-bang weapons platforms and related items: aircraft, rockets, ships, tanks and other combat vehicles, satellites, and communications and other electronic equipment, along with software, maintenance, training, and upgrades for the foregoing products. In this arena of institutionalized cronyism, the living dead rise from the Cold War graveyard to haunt the halls of Congress whenever the defense-appropriations subcommittees are in session. You might wonder how the military will employ, say, an F/A-22 fighter, a B-2 bomber, or an SSN-774 attack submarine to protect you from a suitcase nuke or a vial of anthrax slipped into the country along with the many shipments of contraband goods that enter unseen by government agents. But never mind; just keep repeating: there is a connection between the war on terrorism and the hundreds of billions being spent on useless Cold War weaponry. It's important to Congress, the Pentagon, and the big contractors that you make this connection.

As for the Christian (dispensationalist) soldiers marching onward as to war—in this case, it's more than a metaphor—in order to ease the worries of "God's chosen people" about Israel's hostile neighbors or to hasten the glorious mayhem of the prophesied "end times," suffice it to say that these fundamentalists worked hard to elect their favorite man to the presidency, and they succeeded in doing so. Indeed, one can scarcely imagine a viable national politician who would come closer to satisfying this interest group than George W. "Faith-Based" Bush.

In sum, when we ask ourselves who took the United States to war in Iraq (and keeps it engaged there) and what those individuals hoped to gain by doing so, we quickly come to appreciate what a roaring success this venture has been and continues to be for all of them. In view of the endless death and destruction being visited upon the hapless people of Iraq, however, not to mention the great and growing number of deaths, injuries, and mental disorders being suffered by U.S. troops in the Mesopotamian killing fields, we might well describe this adventure as a catastrophic success.

Acknowledgments

Each entry is dated according to when the essay first appeared. Within each section, items are arranged chronologically.

CRISIS AND LEVIATHAN, AGAIN

"Glory Days for Government: An Economic Historian Talks about National-Security Crises and the Growth of Government" (Interview of Robert Higgs by Michael Lynch), *Reason Online* (September 20, 2001), at http://www.reason.com/ml/ml092001.html. Also appeared as "How Crises Feed Government Growth," *National Post* (Canada), September 28, 2001.

"Crisis Policymaking: Immediate Action, Prolonged Regret," National Center for Policy Analysis *Brief Analysis No. 375*, October 4, 2001; also available at: http://www.ncpa.org/pub/ba/ba375/.

"Wake Up to the Law of the Ratchet: National Emergencies Attract Opportunists Who Seek to Profit from the Growth of Government, Say Steve Hanke and Robert Higgs," *Financial Times* (London), November 26, 2001; also posted by the Independent Institute at http://www.independent.org/newsroom/article.asp?ID=398.

"Every Step We Take" (contribution to the symposium "Guarding the Home Front: Will Civil Liberties Be a Casualty in the War on Terrorism?), *Reason* (December 2001): 38–39; also available at: http://reason.com/0112/fe.symposium.shtml (scroll down).

"Crisis-Induced Losses of Liberty" (letter to the editor), *Wall Street Journal,* January 31, 2002. Reprinted with permission of *The*

Wall Street Journal © 2002 Dow Jones & Company. All rights reserved.

"Wartime Curbs on Liberty Are Costless? (It Just Ain't So!)," *Ideas on Liberty* 52 (March 2002): 6–7; also posted by the Independent Institute at http://www.independent.org/newsroom/article.asp?ID=1392.

"Benefits and Costs of the U.S. Government's War Making," posted by the Independent Institute, October 7, 2004, at http://www.independent.org/newsroom/article.asp?id=137.

AIRPORT (IN)SECURITY

"Federal Oversight Won't Improve Airport Security," *San Francisco Business Times,* October 26–November 1, 2001, 53; also available online at http://sanfrancisco.bcentral.com/sanfrancisco/stories/2001/10/29/editorial2.htm.

"The Pretense of Airport Security," posted by the Independent Institute, October 23, 2003, at http://www.independent.org/newsroom/article.asp?id=1199. Slightly edited version printed as "Transportation Thuggery: A Nation in Its Stocking Feet; Humiliated Travelers Get Only the Pretense of Airport Security," *San Francisco Chronicle,* December 7, 2003; reprinted in *Security Today* magazine (July 2004).

THE DRAFT

"Will the Draft Rise from the Dead?" posted by LewRockwell.com, November 15, 2001, at http://www.lewrockwell.com/orig/higgs3.html.

"Censored Mail: Robert Higgs's unpublished letter to the *War Street Journal*," posted by LewRockwell.com, April 2, 2002, at http://www.lewrockwell.com/orig/higgs4.html.

THE POLITICAL ECONOMY OF THE MILITARY-INDUSTRIAL-CONGRESSIONAL COMPLEX

"The Cold War: Too Good a Deal to Give Up," *Intervention Magazine* (online), February 27, 2002, at http://www.interventionmag.com; also posted by the Independent Institute at http://www.independent.org/newsroom/article.asp?ID=1208.

"U.S. National Security: Illusions versus Realities," posted by LewRockwell.com, July 2, 2002, at http://www.lewrockwell.com/orig/higgs6.html; also posted by the Independent Institute at http://www.independent.org/newsroom/article.asp?id=135.

"The Government Needs to Get Its Own Accounting House in Order," posted by the Independent Institute, July 9, 2002, at http://www.independent.org/newsroom/article.asp?id=425.

"Nation Trembles as Congress Reassembles," posted by LewRockwell.com, September 5, 2002, at http://www.lewrockwell.com/orig/higgs8.html.

"If We're Really in Danger, Why Doesn't the Government Act as if We're in Danger?" posted by LewRockwell.com, October 28, 2002, at http://www.lewrockwell.com/higgs/higgs12.html; also posted by the Independent Institute at http://www.independent.org/newsroom/article.asp?id=114.

"Free Enterprise and War, a Dangerous Liaison," posted by the Independent Institute, January 22, 2003, at http://www.independent.org/tii/news/030122Higgs.html. Edited version printed as "Robert Higgs: Market's Dangerous Liaison with War," *Providence Journal*, February 22, 2003.

"War Prosperity: The Fallacy That Won't Die," a letter sent to the *Wall Street Journal*, posted by the Independent Institute, February 6, 2003, at http://www.independent.org/tii/news/030206Higgs.html; also posted as "The Myth of War Prosperity" by LewRockwell.com, at http://www.lewrockwell.com/higgs/higgs16.html.

"Suppose You Wanted to Have a Permanent War," posted by the Independent Institute, June 12, 2003, at http://www.independent.org/newsroom/article.asp?id=1138. Slightly edited version printed as "All War All the Time: The Battle on Terrorism Is an Excuse to Make Fighting Permanent," *San Francisco Chronicle,* July 6, 2003.

"How Does the War Party Get Away with It?" posted by the Independent Institute, August 25, 2003, at http://www.independent.org/newsroom/article.asp?id=1178. Slightly edited version printed as "The War Party's Enablers: All of Us," *San Francisco Chronicle,* September 14, 2003.

"The Defense Budget Is Bigger Than You Think," posted by the Independent Institute, December 22, 2003, at http://www.independent.org/newsroom/article.asp?id=1258. Printed as "Billions More for Defense—and We May not Even Know It. Good Guess: Double the Pentagon Budget," *San Francisco Chronicle,* January 18, 2004.

BUSH AND THE BUSHIES

"The President Is Reading a Book, I'm Afraid," posted by LewRockwell.com, August 28, 2002, at http://www.lewrockwell.com/orig/higgs7.html; also posted by the Independent Institute, at http://www.independent.org/newsroom/article.asp?id=128. Reprinted in *Spectator* magazine, September 4, 2002.

"George Bush's Faith-Based Foreign Policy," posted by the Independent Institute, February 10, 2003, at http://www.independent.org/newsroom/article.asp?id=443. Slightly edited version printed as "Impending War in Iraq: George Bush's Faith-Based Foreign Policy," *San Francisco Chronicle,* February 13, 2003.

"On Crackpot Realism: An Homage to C. Wright Mills," posted by LewRockwell.com, February 19, 2003, at http://www.lewrockwell.com/higgs/higgs14.html; also posted by the Independent Institute at http://www.independent.org/newsroom/article.asp?id=798.

"Camelot and the Bushies: Some Disturbing Parallels," posted by the Independent Institute, March 7, 2003, at http://www.independent.org/newsroom/article.asp?id=806.

"Is Bush Unhinged?" posted by LewRockwell.com, March 22, 2004, at http://www.lewrockwell.com/higgs/higgs24.html; also posted by the Independent Institute at http://www.independent.org/newsroom/article.asp?id=1267.

THE ROAD TO WAR

"Iraq and the United States: Who's Menacing Whom?" posted by the Independent Institute, August 5, 2002, at http://www.independent.org/newsroom/article.asp?id=118.

"Helplessly, We Await the Catastrophe Our Rulers Are Creating," posted by LewRockwell.com, September 23, 2002, at http://www.lewrockwell.com/higgs/higgs9.html; also posted by the Independent Institute at http://www.independent.org/newsroom/article.asp?ID=430.

"To Make War, Presidents Lie," posted by LewRockwell.com, October 1, 2002, at http://www.lewrockwell.com/higgs/higgs10.html; also posted by the Independent Institute at http://www.independent.org/newsroom/article.asp?id=134. Slightly edited version printed as "The Oval Office Liar's Club," *San Francisco Chronicle,* November 24, 2002. Printed in *Providence Journal,* December 6, 2002, at http://www.projo.com/opinion/contributors/content/projo_20021206_webwar6.2e918.html. Printed in *Providence Journal,* January 31, 2003, at http://www.projo.com/opinion/contributors/content/projo_20030131_31ctwar.2dbdc.html. Excerpts recorded for the "Talking History" program, made available by the Organization of American Historians for broadcast by public-radio stations nationwide.

"Saddam Hussein Can't Blackmail Us with a Fissionable Softball," posted by LewRockwell.com, October 11, 2002, at http://www. lewrockwell.com/higgs/higgs11.html; also posted by the Independent Institute at http://www.independent.org/newsroom/ article.asp?id=131.

"Why the Rush to War?" posted by the Independent Institute, January 23, 2003, at http://www.independent.org/newsroom/article. asp?id=341.

"Paul Craig Roberts Interviews Robert Higgs on War and Liberty," posted by VDARE.COM, February 1, 2003, at http://www. vdare.com/roberts/interview.htm.

"Nuke France," posted by LewRockwell.com, February 22, 2003, at http://www.lewrockwell.com/higgs/higgs15.html.

SLAUGHTERING THE INNOCENT

"Collateral Damage: Two Venues, One Logic," posted by LewRockwell.com, April 11, 2002, at http://www.lewrockwell.com/orig/ higgs5.html. Slightly edited version printed as "Amoral Logic of 'Collateral Damage,'" *San Francisco Examiner,* April 18, 2002; posted by the Independent Institute at http://www.independent.org/newsroom/article.asp?id=100.

"Military Precision versus Moral Precision," posted by the Independent Institute, March 23, 2003, at http://www.independent.org/ newsroom/article.asp?id=1154.

"Some Are Weeping, Some Are Not," posted by LewRockwell.com, April 26, 2003, at http://www.lewrockwell.com/higgs/higgs18. html; also posted by the Independent Institute at http://www. independent.org/newsroom/article.asp?id=1149.

"Are Pro-war Libertarians Right?" posted by LewRockwell.com, May 2, 2003, at http://www.lewrockwell.com/higgs/higgs19. html; also posted by the Independent Institute slightly edited as "Facing the Consequences of the U.S. War in Iraq," at http://www.independent.org/newsroom/article.asp?id=1146.

"Not Exactly an Eye for an Eye," posted by the Independent Institute, June 13, 2003, at http://www.independent.org/newsroom/article.asp?id=1053. Slightly edited version printed in *San Francisco Chronicle*, June 23, 2003.

"Defense of Your Home Is Not Terrorism, Not Even in Iraq," posted by the Independent Institute, July 2, 2003, at http://www.independent.org/newsroom/article.asp?id=1131.

"What's So Special about Those Killed by Hijackers on September 11, 2001?" posted by LewRockwell.com, September 13, 2003, at http://www.lewrockwell.com/higgs/higgs21.html.

"The Crimes at Abu Ghraib Are Not the Worst," posted by LewRockwell.com, May 10, 2004, at http://www.lewrockwell.com/higgs/higgs25.html; also posted by the Independent Institute at http://www.independent.org/newsroom/article.asp?id=1305.

"Has the U.S. Government Committed War Crimes in Afghanistan and Iraq?" posted by the Independent Institute, May 23, 2004, at http://www.independent.org/newsroom/article.asp?id=1311.

CAKE WALK

"WMD Blues" (lyrics), posted by LewRockwell.com, August 15, 2003, at http://www.lewrockwell.com/higgs/higgs20.html.

"Taking Stock One Year after the U.S. Invasion of Iraq," posted by LewRockwell.com, March 18, 2004, at http://www.lewrockwell.com/higgs/higgs23.html; also posted by the Independent Institute at http://www.independent.org/newsroom/article. asp?id=1275.

"Can Bullets and Bombs Establish Justice in Iraq?" posted by the Independent Institute, April 8, 2004, at http://www.independent.org/newsroom/article.asp?id=1284. Excerpt printed in the *San Francisco Chronicle,* May 16, 2004.

"Bush's Iraq War: An Offer You Would Have Refused," posted by the Independent Institute, October 25, 2004, at http://www.independent.org/newsroom/article.asp?id=1407.

"The Iraq War—A Catastrophic Success," posted by the Independent Institute, December 21, 2004, at http://www.independent.org/newsroom/article.asp?id=1441.

Further Reading

Bacevich, Andrew J. 2005. *The New American Militarism: How Americans Are Seduced by War.* New York: Oxford University Press.

Bamford, James. 2004. *A Pretext for War: 9/11, Iraq, and the Abuse of America's Intelligence Agencies.* New York: Doubleday.

Bovard, James. 2003. *Terrorism and Tyranny: Trampling Freedom, Justice, and Peace to Rid the World of Evil.* New York: Palgrave Macmillan.

Denson, John V., ed. 1997. *The Costs of War: America's Pyrrhic Victories.* New Brunswick, N.J.: Transaction.

Eggen, Dan. 2003. Patriot Act Used for More than Anti-terror; Justice Report also Reveals 50 Secretly Detained after 9/11. *San Francisco Chronicle,* May 21 (reprinted from the *Washington Post*).

Eland, Ivan. 2004. *The Empire Has No Clothes: U.S. Foreign Policy Exposed.* Oakland, Calif.: The Independent Institute.

Hentoff, Nat. 2003. *The War on the Bill of Rights and the Gathering Resistance.* New York: Seven Stories Press.

Higgs, Robert. 1987. *Crisis and Leviathan: Critical Episodes in the Growth of American Government.* New York: Oxford University Press.

———, ed. 1990. *Arms, Politics, and the Economy: Historical and Contemporary Perspectives.* New York: Holmes and Meier for the Independent Institute.

————. 1994. The Cold War Economy: Opportunity Costs, Ideology, and the Politics of Crisis. *Explorations in Economic History* 31 (July): 283–312.

————. 2004. *Against Leviathan: Government Power and a Free Society.* Oakland, Calif.: Independent Institute.

Johnson, Chalmers. 2004. *The Sorrows of Empire: Militarism, Secrecy, and the End of the Republic.* New York: Metropolitan.

Kwitney, Jonathan. 1984. *Endless Enemies: The Making of an Unfriendly World.* New York: Penguin.

Leebaert, Derek. 2002. *The Fifty-Year Wound: The True Price of America's Cold War Victory.* Boston: Little, Brown.

Lichtblau, Eric. 2003. Patriot Act's Reach Has Gone beyond Terrorism. *Seattle Times,* September 28 (reprinted from the *New York Times*).

Linfield, Michael. 1990. *Freedom under Fire: U.S. Civil Liberties in Times of War.* Boston: South End Press.

Lobe, Jim. 2003a. How Neo-cons Influence the Pentagon. *Asia Times,* August 8. Available at: http://www.atimes.com/atimes/Middle_East/EH08Ak01.html.

————. 2003b. The Neocon Web. December 23. Available at: http://www.lewrockwell.com/ips/lobe40.html.

Kwiatkowski, Karen. 2004. The New Pentagon Papers: A High-Ranking Military Officer Reveals How Defense Department Extremists Suppressed Information and Twisted the Truth to Drive the Country to War. *Salon,* March 10. Available at: http://www.salon.com/opinion/feature/2004/03/10/osp_moveon.

Porter, Bruce D. 1994. *War and the Rise of the State: The Military Foundations of Modern Politics.* New York: Free Press.

Index

Abbas, Ali Ismail, 165, 185

Abbas, Jamal, 186

Abu Gharaib prisoner abuse, 183–84, 188–89

accountability of federal administrators, 35–36, 58, 130, 183–89

accounting practices, DoD and corporate compared, 56–57, 59–61

Adams, John Quincy, 127

AEI (American Enterprise Institute), 73, 89–90

Afghanistan
    civil death toll, 156, 171–73, 195
    distinguishing friend from foe, 156–57
    as example of freedom, 120–21
    invasion and reconstruction of, 84, 95, 155–57, 171
    U.S. war crimes in, 192–93, 195

Against Leviathan (Higgs), 28

Agriculture Department, 67–68, 69, 70

airline screening industry, 38–40

airport (in)security, 35–40

Albright, Madeleine, 217

American Enterprise Institute (AEI), 73, 89–90

Americans' kicking-ass mentality, 89–90.
    See also society

Andrews, Edmund L., 176

Ashcroft, John, 22, 40, 131

Associated Press (AP), 172–73, 194–95

Auden, W. H., 129

audits, DoD and, 56–57, 60–61

autocratic government, 88

B-2 bomber, 52, 227

Bagram Air Base, Afghanistan, 156

balance-of-payments adjustments, IMF and, 16

ballistic-missile-defense system, 52, 69

Barone, Michael, 21

Baruch, Bernard, 75

Bay of Pigs invasion, 112, 113

Ben-Gurion, David, 99

bin Laden, Osama, 120, 171

bombs and bomb targets
    area of lethal damage, 160–62
    Bush's defense of bombing Baghdad, 162
    cluster bombs and bomblets, 163–64, 168, 173, 185
    JDAMs, 160
    as only option, 108, 109
    as Rumsfeld's form of humanity, 159
    smart bombs, 129–30, 159–62
    See also collateral damage

Bremer, Paul, 212–13

Bretton Woods agreement (1944), 16

Bulletin of the Atomic Scientists, 150

Bundy, McGeorge, 111

Bush, G. W.
    "a new kind of war," 13, 43–44, 69–70, 117–19, 193
    Abu Gharib, best way to ignore, 186
    airport security smokescreen, 38, 40
    on bombings in Madrid, 117
    character of, 100, 143–44, 188
    Congress and, 28–30, 88, 105, 130–31, 207–8, 225

Bush, G. W. (*cont.*)
    defense of bombing Baghdad, 162
    faith-based initiatives, 65, 103
    hiring and firing power for DHS,
        64–65
    intelligence agencies and, 115–16,
        142–43, 203–5
    intelligence of, 99–100, 137
    on Iraqi's return to normal life, 175
    motive for Iraq invasion, 127, 137,
        204–5, 223–27
    9/11 terrorist attacks as boost to, 92,
        180–81
    post-Iraq War pride, 169–70, 173,
        204–5
    on price of Iraq invasion, 218
    public opinion polls, 84
    on terrorist threat, 67, 69–70, 117–18,
        204–5
    torturing the truth, xvi, 113, 115–16,
        133–36, 204–5, 209
    war crimes of, 184–85, 186, 193–96
    world view (nothing-but-good vs.
        nothing-but-evil), 118–20, 131
    See also preemptive war doctrine; war
        on terrorism
Bush, G. W., administration
    Kennedy administration compared to,
        114–16
    "National Security Strategy of the
        United States of America," 103,
        114–15, 131
    Powell, Colin, 115–16
    Rice, Condoleeza, 84
    Rove, Karl, 92
    Saddam Hussein and, 145–46
    world domination agenda, 103–5,
        119–20, 181
    See also Cheney, Dick; Rumsfeld,
        Donald
Bush, G. W., foreign policy
    autocratic decision-making process, 88

counterinsurgency, 113–14
    of death and destruction, 207–8
    faith-based, 103–5
    foreign aid as military financing, 94
    insulting allies, 115
    murder, 213–14
    nothing-but-good vs. nothing-but-
        evil, 118–20
    righteous world dominance, 83–84,
        114–15
    targeting Saddam vs. equally culpable
        dictators, 145–46
    of waste, fraud, and brutality, 30–31
    world domination, 103–5, 119–20
    See also preemptive war doctrine;
        entries beginning with "Iraq"
Bush, George H. W., 138
business-government cooperation, 75,
    76–77, 225–27
Butler, Richard, 126
Butler, Smedley D., 70–71
Byrd, Robert, 65

Caesar, president of U.S. as, 29–31, 88
Cassel, Douglas W., Jr., 173
Castro, Fidel, 112
casualties of warfare, 87
The Causes of World War Three (Mills), 107
CBS News/New York Times poll, 217–18
censorship during wartime, 10–11, 12,
    23–26
Chafee, Lincoln, 127
Cheney, Dick
    as architect of war, 87, 104, 143, 169,
        181, 206–7
    on Iraq War success story, 223, 224
    on new normalcy, 26, 83
    political shrewdness, 111, 115
Chirac, Jacques, 149–51
Christianizing (uplifting) Filipinos,
    133–34
Churchill, Winston, 99

civil liberties violations
Abu Gharaib prisoner abuse, 183–84,
188–89
crisis-induced, 5, 21–22
Red Scare post-WWI, 5–6
U.S. sponsored, in Iraq, 175–77, 220
See also collateral damage
civilian murders. *See* collateral damage
Clemenceau, Georges, 99, 101
cluster bombs and bomblets, 163–64, 168,
173, 185
Cohen, Eliot A., 99–101
COINTELPRO operation, FBI's, 22, 84
Cold War
DoD continuing involvement in,
49–53, 55
domestic surveillance during, 26
government spending for, 13, 69
JFK and, 112–13
nuclear arsenals, USSR and Iraq's
compared, 137
politics of maintaining, 81
war on terrorism as replacement for,
82–86
"The Cold War Is Over, but U.S. Preparation for It Continues" (Higgs), 49
collateral damage (murder of civilians)
in Afghanistan, 156–57, 171–73, 195
civilians–23/target–0, 184–85
in Fallujah, 186–87
immorality of, 161–62, 172–73
leaders' willingness to "pay the price,"
119
in Makr al-Deeb, 194–95
in Nasiriyah, 187–88
with smart bombs, 129–30, 159–62
as unacceptable, 167, 188–89
from unexploded bomblets, 163–64,
168, 173, 185
from using soldiers as rebuilders,
176–77
See also death tolls

community and regional development
funds, 68–69
Congress
Bush's control of, 28–30, 88, 105,
130–31, 207–8, 225
character of members, 63–64, 184
constitutional duties of, 101
dancing with Bush, 207
DHS and member's toes, 64–65
DoD budget and reelection, 53, 85
military oversight and appropriations
committee members, 82
conscientious objectors, imprisonment of,
12, 25
conservatives
as supporters of free enterprise and
warfare state, 73–74, 77
trust in government, 30, 147
Constitution of the United States
Congress relinquishing rights from,
28–30, 88, 105, 130–31, 207–8, 225
degradation of, 29–31
instructions for declarations of war, 101
nullification during crises, 24
sacrificing structure of, 28–30, 130
contingent contracts for public goods,
219–21
contract awards to cronies system, 39, 227.
See also private contractors
corporate accounting practices, 57
corporate income taxes, WWII and, 75–76
counterinsurgency, JFK's policy of, 113–14
crackpot realism, 107–9, 113–15
crimes against humanity, 191, 193, 194–96.
See also collateral damage
crimes against peace, 191, 193–94
crises, society's insecurities and, 81–82
Crisis and Leviathan (Higgs), xiii, 3, 28
Cuban missile crisis, 112, 113

Dao, James, 53
Davis, Bob, 79

death tolls
    Afghan civilians, 156, 171–73, 195
    daily, in America, 179–80
    Iraqi civilians, 172–73, 195
    9/11 terrorist attacks, 171
DeFazio, Peter, 40
Defense Department (DoD)
    accounting practices, 56–57, 59–61
    ballistic-missile-defense system, 52, 69
    budget (2003), 69
    Cold War, continuing preparation for, 49–53, 55
    Hart-Rudman Commission critique of, 50
    Iraq War budget, 218
    nonaccountability of, 58
    objective of, 55–56
    open purse policy, 52
    purpose of, 50–51, 53
    weapons expenditures, 52–53, 70, 84–85
    See also military budget
democracy
    bamboozlement as effective tool, 27
    in Middle East, 30–31, 104–5, 143, 146, 203–4
    worldwide flowering of, 114–15
Diaz, Dave, 156
DoD. *See* Defense Department
DoE (Department of Energy), 93, 96
domestic surveillance, 4–5, 19, 25–26, 84, 131
Dr. Strangelove (movie), 113
the draft, 43–45
due process, obsolescence of, 29–30, 213
DVA (Department of Veterans Affairs), 94, 96

economic controls
    suppression of liberties with, 25
    WWI, during and after, 11, 74–75
    WWII, during and after, 12, 25–26, 75–76

economic development foreign aid funds, 94
education and training program funds, 68
Eland, Ivan, 52
employee-pensions, Congress and, 65
employment
    the draft instead of, 43–44
    as purchase of Democrats' votes, 38, 40
    WWII and, 79
Energy Department (DoE), 93, 96
Espionage Act (1917), 10

F-22 fighter planes, 69, 227
F/A-18E/F fighters, 69
faith-based foreign policy, 103–5
faith-based initiatives, 65, 103
Fallujah, Iraq, 186–87
Faramarzi, Scheherezade, 194–95
farm lobbies as opportunists, 15
farm subsidies vs. fighting terrorism, 67–68
FBI (Federal Bureau of Investigation)
    COINTELPRO operation, 22, 28
    computer update funding, 68
    domestic surveillance, 4–5, 19, 25–26, 84, 131
    USA PATRIOT Act, 21–22, 30, 84
    WWII growth of, 12, 25
federal administrators' accountability, 35–36, 58, 130, 183–89
Federal Reserve System, inflation-creating by, 10
federalizing airport security, 35–36
Fifth Amendment rights, 29–31
The Fifty-Year Wound (Leebaert), 111–14
First Amendment rights
    Americans' willingness to relinquish, 22
    censorship during wartime, 10–11, 12, 23–26
    civilian surveillance, 5, 6
    founders' intent, 45
    USA PATRIOT Act vs., 21–22, 30, 84

wartime suppression of, 10–11, 23–26, 146–47

Fourth Amendment rights, 29–31

Fox News, 91

France, terrorist threat from, 149–51

Franks, Tommy, 195

free markets, 11, 12, 25–26, 73–77, 74–76

free society, meaning of, 121–22

freedom. *See* civil liberties violations; First Amendment rights

Garner, Jay, 170

Gataa, Akram, 205

GDP (gross domestic product), 9, 79–80

Geneva Convention, quaintness of provisions in, 193

Gerecht, Reuel Marc, 73

Glastris, Paul, 43–44

GNP (gross national product), 12

Gonzales, Alberto R., 193

Göring, Hermann, 196

government

   administrators' accountability, 35–36, 58, 130, 183–89

   citizens' beliefs about, 17

   DoD and audit agencies of, 56–57

   exploitation of 9/11 terrorist attacks, 180–81

   farm subsidies vs. fighting terrorism, 67–68

   federal administrators' accountability, 35–36, 58, 130, 183–89

   growth during crises, 9, 11–12, 15, 21–22

   international economic meddling, 76

   lust for growth and control, 30–31

   repression and censorship by, 23–25

   special interests and, 27–29

   spending spikes, WWI and WWII, 9

   taxation, 12, 25, 75–76, 92

   See also entries beginning with "Bush, G. W."

government surveillance, effect of, 19

Graham, Lindsey, 183

Great Depression, 4, 15

gross domestic product (GDP), 9, 79–80

gross national product (GNP), 12

Hamoodi, Abed Hassan, 184–85

Hanke, Steve, 17

Hart-Rudman Commission, 50

Hashem, Kadem, 187–88

Hassan, Mona, 163

Heatwole, Nathaniel, 37

Herold, Marc W., 161, 172

Higgs, Buck "One Horse," 199–201

Higgs, Robert

   on governmental growth during crises, 3–6

Hijazi, Walid, 164

Holmes, Oliver Wendell, Jr., 24

Homeland Security, Department of (DHS)

   Congress as planning committee, 64–65

   as separate from defense, 93–94, 96

Homeland Security, Office of

   Defense Department and/or, 55

   Hart-Rudman recommendation, 50

Hoover, Calvin, 26, 76

Hoover, Herbert, 75

human rights

   degradation of, 29–31

   in Iraq, 120–22, 175–77

   social leveling as substitute for, 43, 45

   war on terrorism vs., 19

   during World War I, 10–11, 23–24

   See also civil liberties violations; First Amendment rights

Human Rights Watch, 195

Hunter, Duncan, 52

Hussein. *See* Saddam Hussein

IBD/TIPP poll, 181

Ibrahim, Saad, 187

IEDs (improvised explosive devices), 205
IMF (International Monetary Fund), 16
imperial objectives of DoD, 51
improvised explosive devices (IEDs), 205
"In Memory of W. B. Yeats" (Auden), 129
industry
    benefits of war, 91–92, 224
    nationalization of, 10, 12
intelligence agencies
    autocratic government and, 88
    Bush and faulty intelligence, 115–16,
        142–43, 203–5
    dancing with Bush, 207
interest expense for past military
    spending, 95, 96
Interior Department, 16
international economic meddling, 76
International Military Tribunal, 191–92
International Monetary Fund (IMF), 16
international-trade controls, 12
Iran, 214
Iraq
    Bush's assertions about WMDs,
        126–27, 137, 203
    Bush's success from, 223–24
    ethnic, religious, and political
        cauldron of, 143, 146
    U.S. interest in, 125–27, 204
Iraq, U.S. liberation (invasion) of
    as American crusade, 104, 227
    Bush and cronies' joviality about,
        169–70
    Bush's belief in success of, 120–22
    as catastrophic success, 223
    civilian death toll, 172–73
    Constitution of the United States and,
        101
    contingent contract for, 219–21
    decision-making process, 28–30, 88,
        105, 130–31, 207–8, 225
    declaration of end, irrelevance of,
        175–77

intelligence manipulation prior to,
    115–16, 136
lethal damage from smart bombs,
    129–30, 159–62
Middle East (except Israel) resistance
    to, 141–42
price paid and value received, 217–19
results of, 205–7
unexploded cluster bomblets, 163–64,
    168, 173, 185
U.S. government propaganda, 167–68,
    177, 186
See also collateral damage
Iraq, U.S. rebuilders (soldiers) in
    damaged bodies and minds of, 87,
        218–19
    inhumanity of, 187
    military conscription, 43–45
    overaggressive tactics, xvi, 175–77,
        194–95, 205
    paying costs of war with, 70, 99, 206,
        227
    as targets of opportunity, 176, 206
    training of, 121, 175–77, 186
Iraq, U.S. restoration (occupation) of
    Abu Gharaib prisoner abuses, 183–84,
        188–89
    as brain surgery with sledge hammers,
        175–76
    Bremer's defense of, 212–13
    costs, financial and human, 218–19
    demonstrations and protests in, 168,
        170
    Iraqi resistance to, 175–77, 212
    post conquest reconstruction, 104–5,
        175–77
Israel, 119–20, 140, 142

Jaffe, Greg, 79
Jamail, Dahr, 186
Jamal, Suha, 164
Japanese, internment of, 12, 25

JDAM (Joint Direct Attack Munition), 160
Johnson, Lyndon Baines, 89, 135
Joint Direct Attack Munition (JDAM), 160
justice
    Bush's devotion to misplaced, 211–12,
        213–14
    waging war vs. establishing, 214–15
Justice Department, 69, 84, 93–94, 96

Kay, David, 208
Kennedy, David M., 135
Kennedy, John F., 111–14
Kerry, John, 207–8
"kicking ass" mentality, 89–90
Kiesling, John Brady, 115
Kim Jong II, 125
Kissim, Daham, 187
Kohler, Horst, 16–17

Landstuhl Regional Medical Center
    (Germany), 206
Leebaert, Derek, 111–14
LeMay, Curtis, 217
libertarians, 28, 31, 169
liberty. *See* civil liberties violations; First
    Amendment rights
Liberty Bonds, 10
Lieberman, Joseph, 65
Lincoln, Abraham, 99
Los Angeles Times, 139
Loy, James, 39–40
Ludlow Resolution, 88
Lugar, Richard, 126
Lynch, Michael, 3–6

Machiavelli, 92
Madison, James, 27
Mahmoud, Amer, 163–64
al-Majid, Ali Hassan, 185
McHale, Stephen, 37
McKiernan, David, 175
McKinley, William, 133–34

McNamara, Robert, 111
McVeigh, Timothy, 155
media
    cooperation of, 88, 91
    dancing with Bush, 207
    marketing war, 91, 167–68, 214
    self-serving rehashing of 9/11 by,
        179–81
Mexican debt crisis, 16
Meyers, Richard, 213
MIC (military-industrial complex), 73–77,
    79, 92. *See also* government contractors
MICC (military-industrial-congressional
    complex), 51–53, 56–57, 82–85
Middle East opposition to invasion of
    Iraq, 141–42
military budget
    as carrot for Democrats, 38, 40
    Cold War, Gulf War, and no war, 49,
        50–51
    for fiscal year 2003, 69
    growth of government and, 6, 15–16
    size of, 93–96, 218
    war on terrorism and, 84–85
military conscription, 43–45
military-industrial complex (MIC), 73–77,
    79, 92. *See also* government contractors
military-industrial-congressional complex
    (MICC), 51–53, 56–57, 82–85
Mills, C. Wright, 107–9
moral rhetoric, 109
morality
    of collateral damage, 157, 161–62,
        172–73
    government propaganda vs., 169, 177,
        180–81
    hard choices and, 168–69
    Rumsfeld's, 159–60
    of smart bombs, 129–30, 159–60
Moskos, Charles, 43–44, 45
Murrah Federal Building, Oklahoma
    City, OK, 155, 180

Mururoa Atoll, South Pacific, 151
Musharraf, Pervez, 140
Muslims, 140, 146, 171, 214

NASA, 96
Nasiriyah, Iraq, 187
National Aeronautics and Space
    Administration (NASA), 96
national debt, 12, 25
National Industrial Recovery Act (1933), 75
national security, illusions vs. realities,
    55–58, 131–32
"National Security Strategy of the
    United States of America" (Bush
    administration), 103, 114–15, 131
nation-building, 104–5
Nawaf, Madhi, 194–95
"A Necessary War" (Gerecht), 73
New York Times, 84, 85, 91, 184–85
news media. *See* media
Nixon, Richard, 16
North Korea, 125, 141
Northrup-Grumman, 52
"Not a Victory for Big Government"
    (Barone), 21
nuclear arsenals
    French, 150–51
    Israeli, 140
    Pakistani, 140
    Russian, 139–40
    US, USSR, and Iraq's compared,
        137–38
Nuclear Posture Review (Bush
    administration), 139
nuclear weapons, 93, 112–13, 137–39
Nuremberg trials, 192

Office of Censorship, 12
oil crises of 1970s, IMF and, 16
O'Neill, Paul, 16–17
opportunists, 15
Oracle Corporation, 91–92

Osprey tilt-rotor aircraft, 69

Pakistan, nuclear arsenal of, 140
patriotism of politicians, 130
payroll withholding of income taxes, 25
peace, the serious people vs., 108–9
Peace Party vs. War Party, 87–88, 92
Perle, Richard. *See* Bush, G. W.,
    administration
Philippine-American War, 133–34
politicians
    character of Congressional, 63–64
    crises responses of, 9
    motive for Iraq invasion, 127, 137,
        204–5, 223–27
    patriotism of, 130, 225
    profits from war, 70–71
    the serious people, 107–9
politics
    of airport security, 38, 40
    capitalizing on "war on terror," 83–86
    crises, taking advantage of, 81–82
    nothing-but-good vs. nothing-but-evil
        world view, 118–20
    special interests, 15, 27–29, 82, 221, 227
    torturing the truth, xvi, 113, 115–16,
        133–36, 204–5, 209
polls. *See* public-opinion polls
Porter, Bruce D., 27, 28
Powell, Colin, 115–16
The Power Elite (Mills), 107
preemptive war doctrine
    Bush administration's faith in, 104–5
    as Bush's path to peace and security,
        114–15
    congressional support for, 130
    for emerging threats [not] fully
        formed, 104, 114
    respect for human life vs., 143–44
    selectiveness of, 125–27
prescription-drug giveaway, Congress
    and, 65

presidential duties under the constitution, 101

private contractors
American imperialism and, 74–75
Cold War–type weaponry for war on terror, 52–53, 69, 85, 227
government bailouts of, 73–77, 82
Iraq War boon, 226–27
TSA and, 38–39

private sector
accounting practices, 57
airport security as, 36
business-government cooperation, 75, 76–77, 225–27
corporations, 57, 75–76, 91–92

Project for the New American Century, 181

prosperity, war vs., 79–80, 147

public ignorance and misplaced trust, xv–xvi, 30, 90–91, 147

public-good via contingent contracts, 219–21

public-opinion polls
Americans' belief in government, 17, 22, 84, 90–91, 181
Americans' public affairs ignorance, 90
on Iraq invasion, 217–18

al Qaeda
false intelligence on Iraq and, 116–18, 136, 203–4
Geneva Convention not applicable to, 193
as justification for murder of innocent civilians, 156–57
Taliban and, 171–72

Qmm Qasr, Iraq, 205

Quadrennial Defense Review (DoD, Oct. 2001), 51

Radi, Khessma, 164–65

railroads, nationalization of, 74–75

Reagan, Ronald, 16

rent controls, New York City, 12, 25–26

Rice, Condoleezza, 84

Richard III (Shakespeare), 196

rights. *See* civil liberties violations; First Amendment rights

Roberts, Paul Craig, 145–47

Roosevelt, Franklin D., 88, 134–35, 181

Roosevelt, Theodore, 100

Rostow, Walter, 111

Rove, Karl, 92

Rumsfeld, Donald
Abu Gharib cover-up, 183
on defense spending, 57–58
on humanity of smart bombs, 159–60
on Iraqi thugs, gangs, and terrorists, 213
political shrewdness, 111
on U.S. shooting of noncombatants, 157
on U.S. use of nuclear weapons, 139

Rusk, Dean, 111

Russert, Tim, 218

Russia, nuclear stockpile in, 139–40

Saddam Hussein, 125–27, 138–39, 145–46, 167

al-Sadr, Muqtada, 212–14

Saudi Arabia, 142

security
and freedom, as oxymoron, 27, 131–32
of Russian nuclear storage facilities, 140

"Security Comes Before Liberty" (Winik), 23, 26

security industry, war on terrorism and, 91–92

Sedition Act (1918), 10, 23–24

September 11, 2001, terrorist attacks
civilian death toll, 171
defense spending post-, 57–58
DoD's expenditures vs. ability to defend against, 50–53

September 11, 2001, terrorist attacks (*cont.*)
 expansion of government due to, 4–5,
  21–22
 Higgs's commentaries on, xiii–xv
 IMF role in aftermath, 16–17
 punishing perpetrators of, 171
 remembrance as self-interested
  exploitation, 179–81
 war on terrorism death toll vs., 172–73
Septi, Rahad, 186
the serious people, 107–9
Shakespeare, William, 196
Sinclair, Upton, 11
Sixth Amendment rights, 29–31
Slaten, Scott, 176
smart bombs, 129–30, 159–62
social insecurity, bolstering of, 81–82, 84, 85
social leveling vs. human liberty, 43, 45
Social Security surplus, 6
society
 "kicking ass" mentality, 89–90
 meaning of freedom in, 121–22
 public ignorance and misplaced trust,
  xv–xvi, 30, 90–91, 147
 the serious people, 107–9
The Sociological Imagination (Mills), 107
Somalia, 105
South Vietnam, 112, 135
Southeast Asia, 112–13, 135
Spanish-American War, 133
special interests, 15, 27–29, 82, 221, 227
Speer, Albert, 196
Stahl, Lesley, 217
State Department, 94, 96
Stonecipher, Harry, 52, 85
Stromberg, Joseph, 103
submarines, Virginia-class attack, 69, 227
The Supreme Command (Cohen), 99–101
Supreme Court, U.S., 24
surveillance activities, 5, 6, 19, 22, 26, 131.
 See also USA PATRIOT Act

Taft, William H., 133
the Taliban, 171–72
Tamimi, Khalid, Amal, and Mayasa, 164,
 185
taxation, 12, 25, 75–76, 92
telephone and telegraph industries,
 nationalization of, 74
Tenet, George "Slam Dunk," 225
terrorism-insurance subsidy, Congress
 and, 65
terrorists and terrorism
 bombing of Baghdad as, 162
 Bush's assurance of stopping, 204
 improvised explosive devices (IEDs),
  205
 opposition to U.S. policies, 119–20, 155
 U.S. policy and increase in, 118,
  121–22, 205
 weapons used against, 52–53, 69, 85,
  227
 weapons used by, 51–52
 See also war on terrorism
Time (magazine), 150
TIPS informants, 131
totalitarianism, 19
Transportation Department, 93–94, 96
Transportation Security Administration
 (TSA), 37–40
Treasury Department, 96
troops. *See* Iraq, U.S. rebuilders (soldiers)
 in
TSA (Transportation Security
 Administration), 37–40
tu quoque defenses, 192
Turkey, 141–42
TV politics, 63–64
Twain, Mark, 63

United Nations, Bush and, 115
United Nations weapons inspectors in
 Iraq, US failure to cooperate with,
  142–43

unlawful combatant, 29
Urabi, Hussain, 164–65
USA PATRIOT Act, 21–22, 30, 84

Vandenberg, Arthur, 81
Veterans Affairs Department (DVA), 94, 96
Vidal, Gore, 155
Vietnam, 112, 135
Von Mises, Ludwig, 80

Wall Street Journal
    advocating violence in Iraq, 214
    on crisis-induced loss of liberties, 21–22
    on defense budget post-9/11, 52–53
    on DoD's weapons expenditures, 85
    as Likud Party megaphone, 89–90
    on security vs. liberty, 23
War and the Rise of the State (Porter), 28
war and wars
    Americans' protests against, 105
    definition and use of term, 109, 118
    Philippine-American War, 133–34
    Vietnam, 112, 135
    See also Iraq, U.S. invasion of;
        preemptive war doctrine; war on
        terrorism; World War I; World
        War II
war crimes
    of Bush, 184–85, 186, 193–96
    definition of, 191–92
    See also collateral damage
War Crimes Act, 193
War Finance Corporation, 4
"War Is a Racket" (Butler), 70–71
war on terrorism
    Bush's "new kind of war," 13, 43–44,
        69–70, 117–19, 193
    citizens' costs, leaders' benefits, 31,
        70–71
    as Cold War replacement, 82–83
    Cold War weapons for, 52–53, 69, 85,
        227

defense spending and, 52–53
    human rights vs., 19
    innocent civilian victims, 171–72
    as new normalcy, 26, 83
    permanence of, 83–86
    as politics vs. ending terrorism, 6–7
    public vigilance, maintaining, 85
    security industry and, 91–92
War Party vs. Peace Party, 87–88, 92
warfare
    censorship and, 10–11, 12, 23–26
    conditions for maintaining
        permanently, 81–86, 88
    continuous, Roosevelt to present,
        28–29
    crackpot realists and, 109, 113–15
    domestic surveillance and, 4–5, 19,
        25–26, 84, 131
    free enterprise and freedom vs., 27, 28,
        73–77, 146–47
    as health of the state, 28, 169, 206
    justice vs., 118
    justification for, 142–43
    news media's marketing of, 91
    as prosperity or numbers game, 79–80,
        147
    public ignorance as fuel for, 90–91
    sacrifices attributable to, 28–29
    as socialistic undertaking, 77
    See also bombs and bomb targets;
        collateral damage; military budget
Washington Post, 17, 194
weapons
    Cold War weapons for war on
        terrorism, 52–53, 69, 85, 227
    DoD weapons expenditures, 52–53,
        70, 84–85
    JDAMs, 160
    See also bombs and bomb targets;
        nuclear arsenals; weapons of mass
        destruction
weapons inspectors in Iraq, 142–43

weapons of mass destruction
   countermeasures, 51
   faulty intelligence on Iraq's, 115–16,
      136, 142–43
   imminent danger from Iraq's, 125–27,
      136, 137, 203–5
   nuclear weapons, 93, 112–13, 137–39
   See also nuclear arsenals
Wheeler, Winslow T., 225
Wilson, Woodrow, 23, 89
Winik, Jay, 23, 26
"WMD Blues" (Higgs), 199–201
Wolfowitz, Paul. *See* Bush, G. W.,
   administration
Wood, David, 160–61
world dominance, righteous, 83–84, 114–15
world domination agenda, 103–5, 119–20
World War I
   government growth for, 9, 24
   governmental controls on business, 11,
      74–75
   human rights during, 10–11, 23–24
   Sedition Act, 10, 23–24
   Wilson's entrance into, 89, 134
   World Finance Corporation, 4
World War II
   economic controls during and after, 12,
      25–26, 75–76
   government growth for, 9, 11–12
   internment of Japanese, 12, 25
   LeMay on firebombing of Tokyo, 217
   Roosevelt's entrance into, 134–35
   U.S. hegemony since, 28–29
   World Finance Corporation, 4
writ of habeas corpus, end of, 29
Wyndham Peaks Resort and Golden Door
   Spa (Telluride, CO), 39

Zogby, John, 22

About the Author

ROBERT HIGGS is Senior Fellow in Political Economy at The Independent Institute and Editor of the Institute's quarterly journal, *The Independent Review: A Journal of Political Economy.* He received his Ph.D. in economics from the Johns Hopkins University, and he has taught at the University of Washington, Lafayette College, and Seattle University. He has been a visiting scholar at Oxford University and Stanford University.

Dr. Higgs is the editor of three Independent Institute books, *Arms, Politics, and the Economy: Historical and Contemporary Perspectives* (1990), *Hazardous to Our Health? FDA Regulation of Health Care Products* (1995), and *Re-Thinking Green: Alternatives to Environmental Bureaucracy* (2005), and of the volume *Emergence of the Modern Political Economy* (1985). His authored books include *The Transformation of the American Economy 1865–1914: An Essay in Interpretation* (1971), *Competition and Coercion: Blacks in the American Economy, 1865–1914* (1977), *Crisis and Leviathan: Critical Episodes in the Growth of American Government* (1987), and *Against Leviathan: Government Power and a Free Society* (2004). A contributor to numerous scholarly volumes, he is the author of more than 100 articles and reviews in academic journals of economics, demography, history, and public policy.

His popular articles have appeared in the *Wall Street Journal, Los Angeles Times, Providence Journal, Chicago Tribune, San Francisco Examiner, San Francisco Chronicle, Society, Reason, AlterNet,* and many other newspapers, magazines, and Web sites, and he has appeared on NPR, NBC, ABC, C-SPAN, CBN, CNBC, PBS, America's Talking Television, Radio America Network, Radio Free Europe, Talk

Radio Network, Voice of America, Newstalk TV, the Organization of American Historians' public radio program, and scores of local radio and television stations. He has also been interviewed for articles in the *New York Times, Washington Post, Al-Ahram Weekly, Terra Libera, Investor's Business Daily,* UPI, *Congressional Quarterly, Orlando Sentinel, Seattle Times, Chicago Tribune, National Journal, Reason, Washington Times,* WorldNetDaily, *Folha de São Paulo,* Newsmax, *Financial Times,* Creators Syndicate, *Insight, Christian Science Monitor,* and many other news media.

Dr. Higgs has spoken at more than 100 colleges and universities and to such professional organizations as the Economic History Association, Western Economic Association, Population Association of America, Southern Economic Association, International Economic History Congress, Public Choice Society, International Studies Association, Cliometric Society, Allied Social Sciences Association, American Political Science Association, American Historical Association, and many others.

INDEPENDENT STUDIES IN POLITICAL ECONOMY

THE ACADEMY IN CRISIS: The Political Economy of Higher Education | *Ed. by John W. Sommer*

AGAINST LEVIATHAN: Government Power and a Free Society | *Robert Higgs*

AGRICULTURE AND THE STATE: Market Processes and Bureaucracy | *E. C. Pasour, Jr.*

ALIENATION AND THE SOVIET ECONOMY: The Collapse of the Socialist Era | *Paul Craig Roberts*

AMERICAN HEALTH CARE: Government, Market Processes and the Public Interest | *Ed. by Roger D. Feldman*

ANTITRUST AND MONOPOLY: Anatomy of a Policy Failure | *D. T. Armentano*

ARMS, POLITICS, AND THE ECONOMY: Historical and Contemporary Perspectives | *Ed. by Robert Higgs*

BEYOND POLITICS: Markets, Welfare and the Failure of Bureaucracy | *William C. Mitchell & Randy T. Simmons*

THE CAPITALIST REVOLUTION IN LATIN AMERICA | *Paul Craig Roberts & Karen LaFollette Araujo*

CHANGING THE GUARD: Private Prisons and the Control of Crime | *Ed. by Alexander Tabarrok*

CUTTING GREEN TAPE: Toxic Pollutants, Environmental Regulation and the Law | *Ed. by Richard Stroup & Roger E. Meiners*

THE DIVERSITY MYTH: Multiculturalism and Political Intolerance on Campus | *David O. Sacks & Peter A. Thiel*

DRUG WAR CRIMES: The Consequences of Prohibition | *Jeffrey A. Miron*

THE EMPIRE HAS NO CLOTHES: U.S. Foreign Policy Exposed | *Ivan Eland*

ENTREPRENEURIAL ECONOMICS: Bright Ideas from the Dismal Science | *Ed. by Alexander Tabarrok*

FAULTY TOWERS: Tenure and the Structure of Higher Education | *Ryan C. Amacher & Roger E. Meiners*

FREEDOM, FEMINISM, AND THE STATE: An Overview of Individualist Feminism | *Ed. by Wendy McElroy*

HAZARDOUS TO OUR HEALTH?: FDA Regulation of Health Care Products | *Ed. by Robert Higgs*

HOT TALK, COLD SCIENCE: Global Warming's Unfinished Debate | *S. Fred Singer*

LIBERTY FOR WOMEN: Freedom and Feminism in the Twenty-First Century | *Ed. by Wendy McElroy*

MARKET FAILURE OR SUCCESS: The New Debate | *Ed. by Tyler Cowen & Eric Crampton*

MONEY AND THE NATION STATE: The Financial Revolution, Government and the World Monetary System | *Ed. by Kevin Dowd & Richard H. Timberlake, Jr.*

OUT OF WORK: Unemployment and Government in Twentieth-Century America | *Richard K. Vedder & Lowell E. Gallaway*

A POVERTY OF REASON: Sustainable Development and Economic Growth | *Wilfred Beckerman*

PRIVATE RIGHTS & PUBLIC ILLUSIONS | *Tibor R. Machan*

RECLAIMING THE AMERICAN REVOLUTION: The Kentucky & Virginia Resolutions and Their Legacy | *William J. Watkins, Jr.*

REGULATION AND THE REAGAN ERA: Politics, Bureaucracy and the Public Interest | *Ed. by Roger Meiners & Bruce Yandle*

RESTORING FREE SPEECH AND LIBERTY ON CAMPUS | *Donald A. Downs*

RE-THINKING GREEN: Alternatives to Environmental Bureaucracy | *Ed. by Robert Higgs and Carl P. Close*

SCHOOL CHOICES: True and False | *John D. Merrifield*

STRANGE BREW: Alcohol and Government Monopoly | *Douglas Glen Whitman*

TAXING CHOICE: The Predatory Politics of Fiscal Discrimination | *Ed. by William F. Shughart, II*

TAXING ENERGY: Oil Severance Taxation and the Economy | *Robert Deacon, Stephen DeCanio, H. E. Frech, III, & M. Bruce Johnson*

THAT EVERY MAN BE ARMED: The Evolution of a Constitutional Right | *Stephen P. Halbrook*

TO SERVE AND PROTECT: Privatization and Community in Criminal Justice | *Bruce L. Benson*

THE VOLUNTARY CITY: Choice, Community and Civil Society | *Ed. by David T. Beito, Peter Gordon & Alexander Tabarrok*

WINNERS, LOSERS & MICROSOFT: Competition and Antitrust in High Technology | *Stan J. Liebowitz & Stephen E. Margolis*

WRITING OFF IDEAS: Taxation, Foundations, & Philanthropy in America | *Randall G. Holcombe*

For further information and a catalog of publications, please contact:
THE INDEPENDENT INSTITUTE
100 Swan Way, Oakland, California 94621-1428, U.S.A.
510-632-1366 · Fax 510-568-6040 · info@independent.org · www.independent.org